Sports Starters

Riding

JANE HOLDERNESS-RODDAM

COLLINS
Glasgow & London

First published 1979
Reprinted with revisions 1982
by William Collins Sons and Company Limited,
Glasgow and London
© 1979 William Collins Sons and Company Limited

Devised, edited and designed by Youé and Spooner Limited

Special photography by John McGovren
Illustrations by Malcolm Studio
Filmset by Photocomp Limited
Colour processing by Medway Reprographic Limited

ISBN 0 00 411610 0
Printed in Spain by Graficromo, S.A. ~ Córdoba

Contents

Introduction

It all started when my mother, in exasperation at my inability to walk at eighteen months old (due entirely to laziness), put me into a basket riding chair on my brother's pony, Tickle. The excitement caused by this experience apparently galvanized me into action and soon I was mobile at the mere mention of Tickle's name. From then on I never looked back.

Coming from a fairly 'horsy' family, with five brothers and sisters, I had plenty of competition to contend with and, despite the inevitable falls, I loved every minute of those early days.

Thanks entirely to the generosity of my sisters who kept my horse going, I was extremely fortunate in being able to continue riding after I started my career as a nurse. I shall never forget the thrill and excitement of going straight from night duty to win the Badminton Horse Trials in 1968 on my little horse Our Nobby. This event led to my being chosen as a member of Great Britain's team which won the gold medal at the Mexico Olympic Games.

Since then I have had successes and of course disappointments. Riding has taken me to many places and through it I have met interesting people and made a lot of friends, and I shall always be grateful to my parents who taught me from the start to take the rough with the smooth.

At three years old I won my first silver cup in a leading-rein class but, on being placed only second at the next show, I demanded a silver cup from the horrified judge and my mortified mother. For the rest of the season I was put on 36-year-old Foxie who was always in the back row and I soon learned my lesson!

I have thoroughly enjoyed compiling this book and, being my first venture into writing, I owe a great deal of gratitude to those more experienced in the publishing world for their hard work, tolerance and kindness. My thanks go particularly to Elaine Peel and Vivienne Kelleway who typed the manuscript from my handwritten notes; to my sister Jennie and her husband Anthony who kindly allowed me to use their stables; to the students at Catherston Stud and to Sarah Drewett, Catherine Bullen, Margaret Hughes, Ed Ivory, Priscilla Leigh and the Wroe family for their help with the special photography; and finally to Lorry Spooner who edited my manuscript and without whose help this book could never have been produced.

I hope that those of you who have never ridden will be encouraged by this book to take up the sport. If you already know the basics, then I hope this book will serve to fire your enthusiasm. For if you have even half as much pleasure as I have had from riding, you will be in for a very enjoyable time. Good luck!

Jane Holderness-Roddam

The author, Jane Holderness-Roddam above, and right, riding Just So in the cross country phase of the Army Horse Trials Three-Day Event at Tidworth, Hampshire

First things first

Starting any new sport or hobby is an exciting proposition. There is so much to discover and learn and the following information will help to start you on your way.

Before you actually commit yourself to riding lessons, it is essential to find out as much as you can about the sport. A visit to your local riding school will show you what is involved. If you have difficulty in locating one, the recreation department of your local authority will normally be able to give you information about the schools in your area, and you can arrange to go along and watch a few lessons so that you become familiar with the procedure.

You may prefer, however, to go out riding in a beginners' group at a school, which will give you an initial experience of riding.

A riding holiday may appeal to you. There are many types from which to choose, some of which cater for the complete beginner and they will give you a first-class introduction to riding and all that it entails.

Yet another way of finding out about riding is to get a job in a stable. You will learn about horses very quickly in this way, as you may be expected to participate in every job, from the more enjoyable activities, such as exercising the horse, to the hard work of mucking out.

Reading about the subject is vital and of course this is where this book comes in. Every aspect of riding is covered to help the beginner to become proficient, from basic information on equipment and tack, mounting and dismounting, the different paces, through to preparation for competitions, owning and caring for a horse. Each subject is covered in great detail and illustrated with photographs and diagrams.

How to begin

One of the first things you will need to know is how to identify the various pieces of the horse's tack. The diagram below shows a horse dressed ready for riding, which in equestrian terms is known as being saddled or tacked up. Study the names of the pieces of the bridle and saddle, so that you will be well informed before you take your first lesson. A full description of the tack is given on pages 18-19.

The illustrations on the following two pages show the parts of the horse, which are known as the points, and again it will help if you know these before you set out. Other terms that you are likely to come across very early on are those used to describe the right and left hand sides of the horse. When you are facing in the same direction as the horse, his right hand side is known as the offside and his left hand side is known as the nearside.

A final piece of advice before you start your venture: do not rush off to buy a lot of equipment until you discover just how seriously you intend to take up the sport. A lot of so-called vital equipment is really quite unnecessary, especially in the early stages. The only essential piece of equipment you will need is a good, safe, well fitting hat. This is described in detail on page 16, along with other riding clothes you may eventually need. Some riding schools provide hats, so you may prefer to borrow from them for the first few lessons.

▼ The diagram shows a horse equipped for riding, wearing a bridle and saddle. In equestrian terms this is known as being saddled or tacked up. A full explanation of all the tack shown is given on pages 18-19

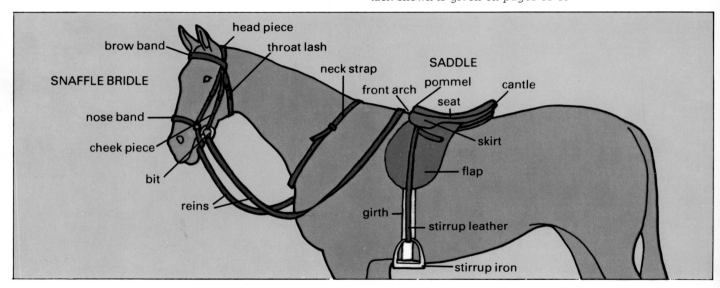

Points of the horse

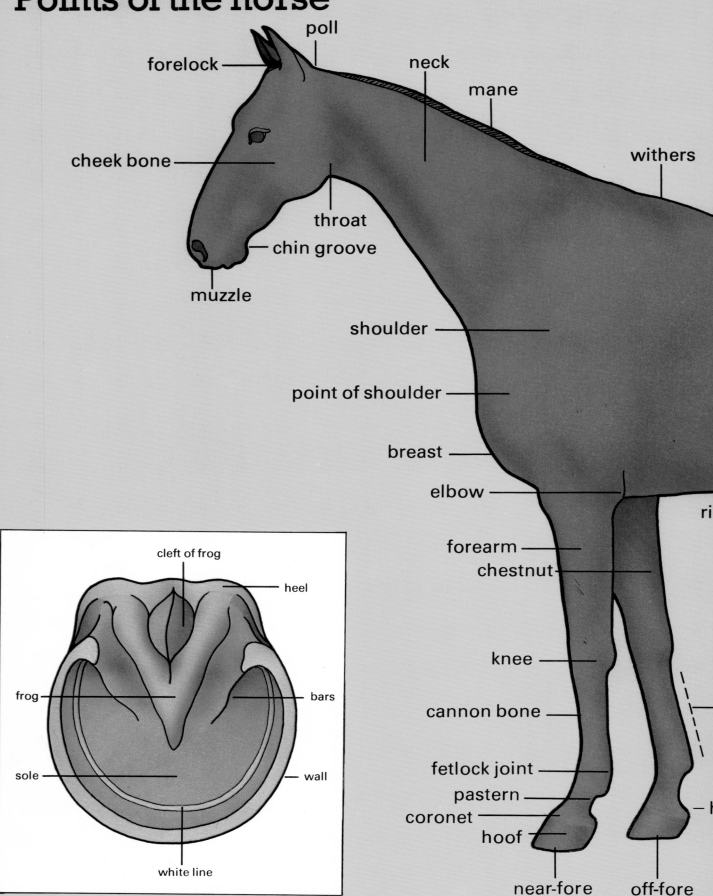

poll

forelock

neck

mane

withers

cheek bone

throat

chin groove

muzzle

shoulder

point of shoulder

breast

elbow

rib

forearm

chestnut

cleft of frog

heel

frog

bars

sole

wall

knee

cannon bone

fetlock joint

pastern

coronet

hoof

white line

near-fore

off-fore

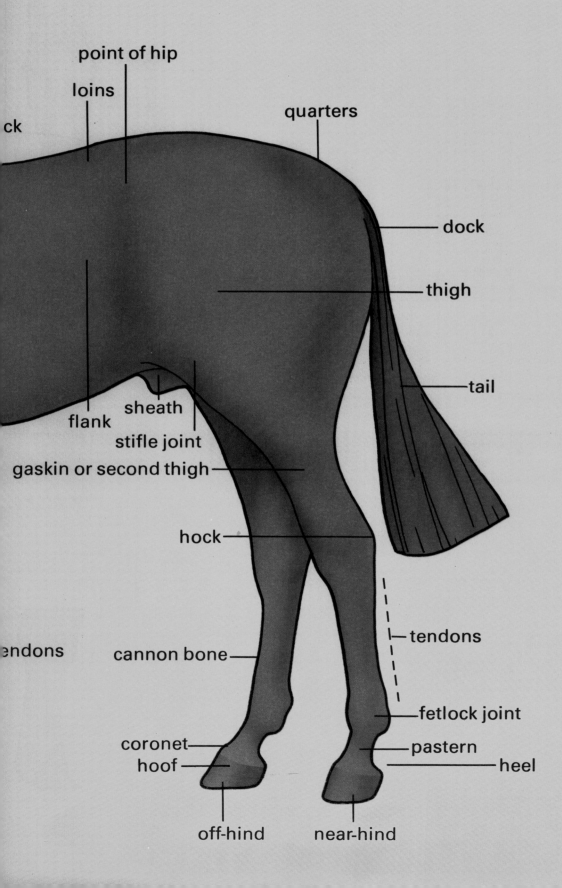

point of hip

loins

ck

quarters

dock

thigh

tail

sheath

flank

stifle joint

gaskin or second thigh

hock

ndons

tendons

cannon bone

fetlock joint

coronet

pastern

hoof

heel

off-hind

near-hind

13

Colours and markings

▲ Horses are measured in metres or hands (a hand being 4in) and the measurement is taken from ground level to the highest point of the withers. Generally speaking, a horse measures 1.52m (15 hands) or over, a pony under this

To describe a horse correctly you need to know something of the terms used. Height measurement forms part of the correct description of the horse and the diagram above shows how the measuring of a horse is carried out.

Special names are given to describe the colours of the horse. 'Points', which are always black, refer to the muzzle, tips of the ears, mane, tail and the extremities of the legs. A bay horse is a reddish brown colour usually with black points. A chestnut is a ginger or reddish colour normally with matching mane and tail. Brown horses are dark brown tending to become black towards the feet. A grey horse has a mixture of black and white hairs. Iron grey describes a horse whose black hairs predominate over white; a light grey has the white hairs predominating; a flea-bitten grey is grey with brownish flecks. A dun horse varies from mouse colour to golden, usually with black points and possibly a list (a dark line down the spine). A palomino is a golden colour with a white mane and tail. Roans are of two kinds: either red or strawberry which is a mixture of bay or chestnut and white hairs; or blue which is brown or black mixed with white hairs. A piebald is black and white; a skewbald is any other colour, usually bay or chestnut, and white.

Horses may have white face and leg markings and the most common types are illustrated.

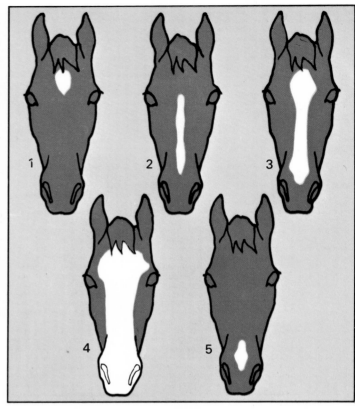

▲ The position and length of the horse's white facial markings determine the names given to them. The most common are shown above and are as follows: **1** A star **2** A stripe **3** A blaze **4** A white face which may also have one or two wall (blue) eyes **5** A snip

The illustrations show the different colours of a horse ▶

▼ The names given to the white markings on the legs generally indicate the parts affected. The three illustrations show: **1** A stocking **2** A sock **3** A coronet. The horse may also have white feet with white leg markings

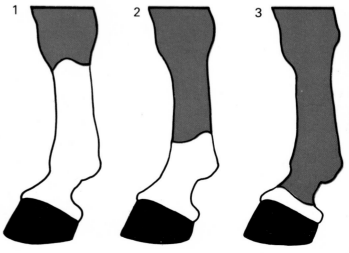

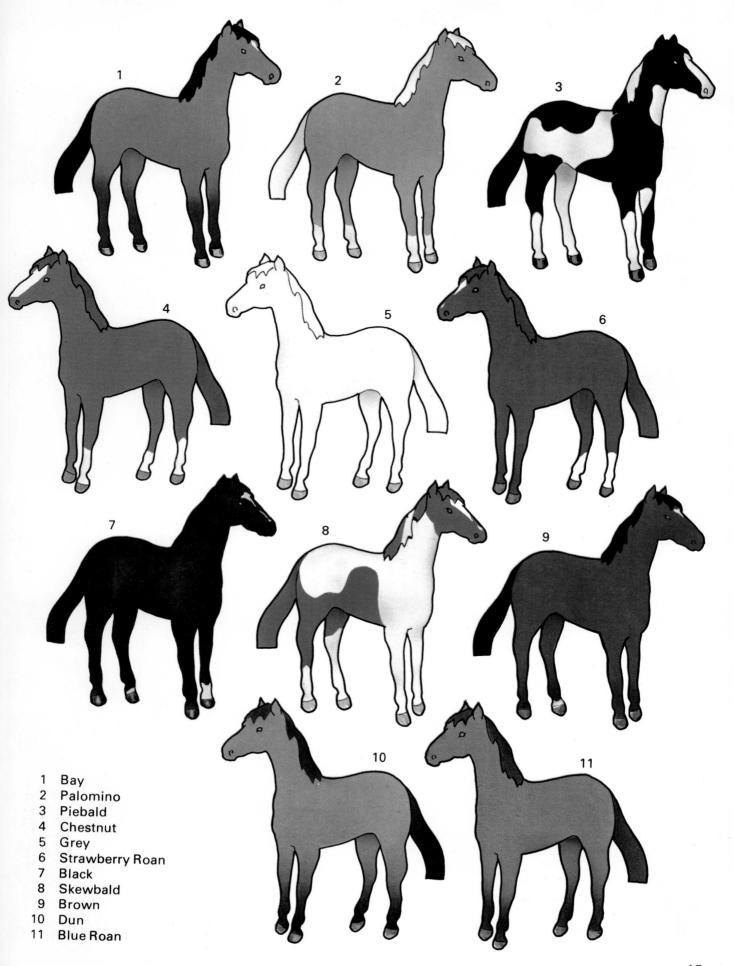

1 Bay
2 Palomino
3 Piebald
4 Chestnut
5 Grey
6 Strawberry Roan
7 Black
8 Skewbald
9 Brown
10 Dun
11 Blue Roan

15

Equipment for the rider

The most important piece of the rider's equipment is a good, well fitting riding hat. It is essential for safety's sake that this is worn at all times when riding.

There are several types of riding hat on the market, ranging from fairly cheap to expensive. The type you need is a hunting cap, a hat well padded inside and with a hard shell. Make sure you choose one that fits your head securely. To ensure it stays firmly in place while you are riding, a piece of black elastic should be sewn on to the hat and fitted either under the hair at the back or under the chin. Alternatively, wear the hat with a safety harness which is illustrated on page 120. This should be attached round the outside of the hat, taken under the chin and adjusted so that it feels secure. The hat should never be placed on the back of the head but should sit squarely, parallel with the ground when the rider is looking straight ahead.

For cross country riding a racing or jockey's crash hat with a coloured silk is usually required. This provides extra protection and is compulsory for horse trials, all forms of racing and several hunter trials. Other hats are the bowler, worn when hunting and in the show ring, and the top hat also worn when hunting, in the show ring

and in more advanced dressage competitions.

Jodhpur boots are the most suitable footwear for riding as they are designed to protect the ankles. Long, leather, hunting boots are also excellent and are well worth the expense for the ambitious rider, as a good pair should last several years if well cared for. Hunting boots are correct dress for adult riders and should always be worn with garters which are leather straps fastened with buckles round the top of the boot. In the early stages a good, strong pair of walking shoes would be suitable so long as they have a heel which cannot slip through the stirrup irons. Nowadays long, rubber riding boots are becoming increasingly popular but rubber soles can stick in the stirrup irons and for this reason Wellington boots with their rough soles are totally unsuitable.

Jodhpurs or breeches are the most comfortable riding wear as they are specially designed for the purpose and have extra padding on the knee. Jodhpurs are full length and worn with jodhpur boots. They are the most popular dress for children. Breeches are designed to be worn with the long hunting boot and are the adult form of dress, although either type can be worn by any age-group except in

▼ Both shoes below are unsuitable for riding. The rough rubber sole of the lace-up is unsafe and because it has no heel, the foot will slip through the stirrup. The heel of the black shoe is too high for the rider to keep the correct foot position and the instep could get stuck in the stirrup

▼ This leather jodhpur boot is the most suitable type of footwear for riding. It has a full, smooth sole and sensible heel and the elasticated sides hidden under the jodhpurs give support to the ankle. The experienced rider has the stirrup iron on the ball of her foot

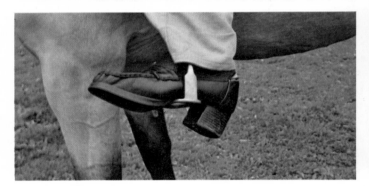

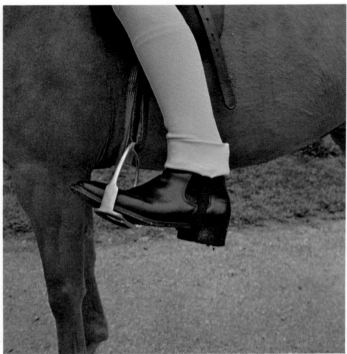

▲ The members of this group are all sensibly and appropriately equipped for riding, wearing jodhpurs, boots and well fitting, hard hats. The straps round the horses' necks and running from the reins down between the fore legs are running martingales, described in detail overleaf

some competitions for which there is a specified code of dress.

For the first few lessons a strong pair of jeans or trousers would be adequate. However, if you find that they do not provide your legs with enough protection against rubbing, wear tights or long underwear beneath them. Children are usually quite happy to wear jeans tucked into socks, with jodhpur boots or walking shoes.

Anoraks or zip-up jackets are adequate for everyday riding. Make sure that whatever type of jacket you choose to wear is buttoned or zipped when you are riding, as a flapping jacket can easily frighten a horse with disastrous consequences. Eventually a proper tweed hacking jacket will be required. This should be a good fit, not too short and of a mellow colour. Large checks or bright, garish colours are considered very unprofessional. A tweed jacket is correct for any form of riding for children or adults but, as you progress, you may feel you would like to have a blue or black hunting coat which is worn in the more advanced events.

Riding clothes are designed to be practical and protective and your choice depends basically on the type of riding you want to do. Certainly to start with you will need only a hat, jodhpurs and boots, and possibly a pair of string or leather gloves. Equipped with these you will feel comfortable and safe.

To be appropriately dressed for any competitive riding you should wear a hat, coat, jodhpurs or breeches, boots, a shirt and tie (the tie secured with a tie-pin), gloves and carry a stick. Children competing in gymkhana events usually wear polo-necked sweaters. For some events, such as long-distance and cross country riding, you may wear a sweater and crash hat but the schedules for the events will usually state the clothing to be worn.

Riding clothes can normally be bought from the sportswear department of big stores, sports shops or from saddlers, many of which have a good second-hand shop. With children growing so quickly, it is often more practical to buy second-hand clothes for them. Do, however, buy a really good hat for your child – it may well save his life if he is involved in an accident. Riding clothes are also often advertised in most of the equestrian magazines but it is usually better to try on the clothes than rely on descriptions and then be disappointed if the article ordered is not what you wanted.

Tack for the horse

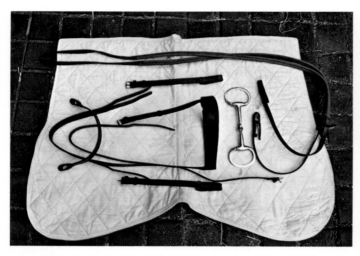

▲ The snaffle bridle, described in detail in the text below, has been taken apart and laid out in such a way as to show clearly the individual pieces and how those pieces fit together when reassembling the bridle

▲ The snaffle bridle has now been reassembled. The type of bit shown is an egg-butt which is the mildest and is therefore gentle on the horse's mouth. The nose band is a cavesson which goes above the bit, approximately two fingers' width below the horse's prominent cheek bone

Your tack must be comfortable and suitable for both horse and rider. To start with it is unnecessary to have more than the basic essentials but when choosing tack it is worth getting the best you can afford, because if it is good and well cared for it should not only last a lifetime but also has second-hand value should you want to change it at any time.

The basic requirements are a head collar and rope or halter, a bridle with bit, a saddle with stirrup irons and leathers, a girth, and a neck strap for the beginner. The diagram showing the horse tacked up is on page 10. If a child is starting with a small pony on which the saddle is liable to slip forward, then a crupper (illustrated on page 21) is very useful. This is a strap which goes under the pony's tail at one end and attaches at the other end to the metal D-shaped ring on the back of the saddle.

A head collar (illustrated on page 71) is usually made of leather or nylon and you will need to buy a rope to attach to it. A halter (illustrated on page 86) is a head collar and rope all in one, made of webbing. Both are used for leading or tying up the horse.

The bridle must be of the right size for your horse and fitted with a suitable bit of a comfortable size. A snaffle bridle with an egg-butt bit is the best type, as the bit is the mildest and is therefore gentle on the horse's mouth. The bridle consists of a head piece and throat lash made of the same piece of leather; a brow band which goes on to the head piece and prevents it from slipping back; two cheek pieces attached at one end to the head piece and at the other end

to the bit; a nose band on its own head piece (this may be a cavesson which lies above the bit, or a dropped nose band which when fastened has the front strap above the nostrils and the back strap below the bit fitting into the horse's chin groove, see page 24 for illustrations of both these types); a bit which is attached to the cheek pieces; and reins attached to the bit and having a centre buckle. Some of the different types of bridle and bit are explained and illustrated on pages 24 and 106.

A strap to fit loosely round the horse's neck is an extremely useful piece of equipment for the beginner, as it can be used to hold on to and so help him to keep his balance. This may be either an old stirrup leather or the neck strap from a martingale.

There are three types of martingale: the running martingale, the standing martingale and the Irish martingale.

The one in most common use is the running martingale which helps to prevent the horse from throwing his head up and beyond the point of control. It consists of two straps, as shown laid out in the photograph above right and on the horses in the photograph on the previous page. One strap goes through the horse's fore legs and attaches at the looped end to the girth, and the buckle allows for adjustment. The other end divides into two pieces each of which has a ring at the end through which the reins pass. This strap is attached to and supported by the second strap which goes round the horse's neck.

The martingale is adjusted to the correct length if, when attached to the girth, the rings at

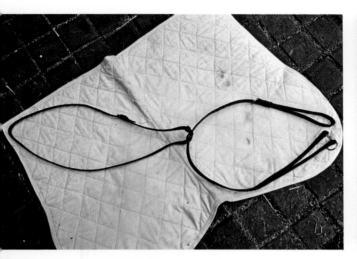

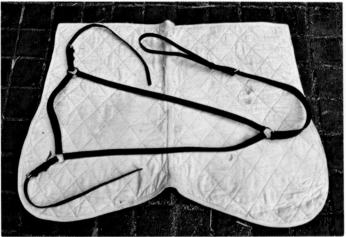

▲ The running martingale is used to prevent the horse from throwing his head up and beyond the point of control. The reins are passed through the rings at one end and the other end is attached to the girth. This strap is attached to and supported by the second strap which goes round the neck

▲ The breastplate is used to prevent the saddle from slipping back. It fits round the horse's neck and the two loose ends are attached to the front D-rings on the saddle. The other strap goes through the horse's fore legs and is attached at its looped end to the girth

the other end just reach the horse's withers. Rubber or leather stops should be put on the reins to prevent the rein buckles from getting caught on the rings of the martingale.

The standing martingale is used for the same purpose as the running martingale but is generally considered nowadays to be too restricting on the horse's head. It is similar in design to the running martingale in that it has two straps, one of which is the neck strap. The other strap attaches at one end to the girth but it is the other end of this strap which differs from that of the running martingale. Instead of having rings through which the reins pass, it has a looped end which attaches to a cavesson nose band.

The Irish martingale is used mainly in racing and prevents the reins from going over the horse's head. It is simply a short strap with a ring at each end through which the reins pass, so that the strap keeps the reins together.

The breastplate, illustrated above right, is used to prevent the saddle from slipping back. It consists of a neck strap with two short straps which go through the D-rings on the front of the saddle and are attached by buckles. The other strap goes through the fore legs and attaches to the girth to keep the breastplate in place.

The saddle is the most expensive but important part of your tack. It must be carefully chosen to ensure it fits you and the horse correctly and comfortably. A general-purpose saddle is best for every day and should help to put the rider in a good position. Experienced guidance on the choice of it will prove invaluable

and a saddler will always give advice.

There must be a clear channel between the saddle and the horse's spine, not so wide that it comes down on to the horse's withers nor so narrow that it pinches the horse. Above all, it must rest comfortably on the horse with the weight evenly distributed on the back muscles. The saddle should be tried with the rider mounted. Saddles are discussed in more detail on page 25.

It is sometimes virtually impossible to get a saddle that sits properly on very small ponies and a felt pony pad (illustrated on the next page) is often the answer. This is a saddle without a tree (the beechwood frame on which conventional saddles are built). It usually needs a crupper to keep it in place and two girths should be used for safety.

The stirrup irons should be the right size for your foot. If they are too narrow or small, your foot could get caught; too large and your foot could slip through. Stainless steel is safest for stirrup irons – indeed for all tack. Pure nickel is not advisable as it is soft and liable to snap.

Stirrup leathers should be of the right width to fit easily through the irons and of sufficient length to be adjusted for different types of riding.

Girths should be of the right length for the horse or pony. When they are on the horse, the buckles should be level and there should be at least three holes on each side to take up. There are several different varieties of girth on the market; leather, string and nylon are all good and strong. Webbing girths are apt to snap, so are not to be recommended.

Saddling up

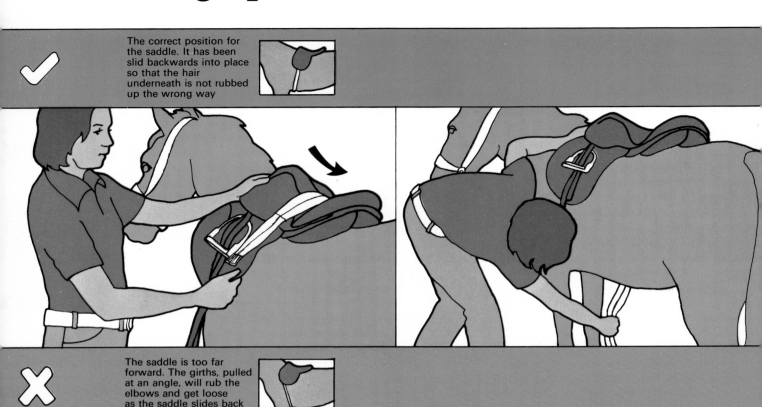

The correct position for the saddle. It has been slid backwards into place so that the hair underneath is not rubbed up the wrong way

The saddle is too far forward. The girths, pulled at an angle, will rub the elbows and get loose as the saddle slides back

▲ The saddle has been placed gently on the horse's back, well forward on the withers, and is now being slid backwards into position. The girths have already been attached to the offside girth straps and are laid across the saddle, and the stirrup irons are up

▲ The girths have been let down from the saddle and the rider is now drawing them up under the horse, making sure as she does so that they are not twisted or crossed. She must take care, when reaching for the girths, not to bend underneath the horse. He may kick out suddenly, at a fly for instance, and cause her severe injury

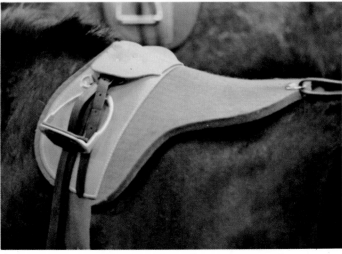

▲ When a conventional saddle will not sit properly on a small pony, a felt pony pad is often the answer. The front of this one is lined with leather and a crupper is attached to prevent it from slipping forward. The stirrup irons are up while the rider is off the pony

Before you start to saddle up, put a head collar or halter on the horse and tie him up firmly so that he cannot wander around or tread on you. The saddle should already have the girths attached to the offside girth straps situated under the saddle flaps and be laid across the seat, and the stirrup irons should be up, as shown in the diagrams.

Approach the horse quietly towards his shoulder and place the saddle gently on his back well forward on the withers, then slide it backwards into place. This ensures that the hair is not rubbed up the wrong way. Let the girths slowly down from the saddle, taking care that they do not knock against the horse's legs in the process. Bend down and take hold of the girths, bring them through under the horse and attach them to the girth straps. The buckles should be level on both sides of the saddle and the girths tight enough to hold the saddle firmly. Check and tighten the girths again before mounting and

The correct fit on the horse. There is enough room to slide two fingers between the withers and the saddle's front arch

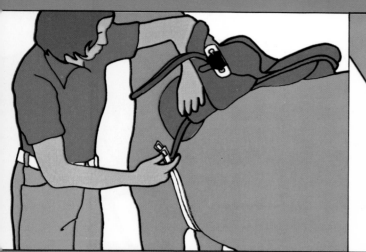

Because the saddle is too low on the horse it is pressing down on the withers and will cause soreness

▲ While the girths are being attached to the girth straps the right forearm keeps the saddle flap up out of the way. The girths should not be fastened too tightly. They should just hold the saddle firmly at this stage but should be checked and tightened again before the rider mounts

▲ The saddle is on, in the correct position and the girths are done up. Before mounting, the rider must ensure that the girth guards are well down, as these protect the saddle flaps from being marked and worn by the buckles of the girths, and that the pommel is not pressing on the horse's withers. If it is, a pad should be placed under the front of the saddle, as a temporary measure

inspect both sides to see that the girth guards are well down over the buckles, thus preventing the saddle flaps from getting marked or worn.

It is important to check that the pommel does not come down on the withers. If it does, a pad made from a folded stable rubber (see page 100) could be used as a temporary measure. Make sure it is pulled well up under the front of the saddle. Then, at the first opportunity, take the saddle for re-stuffing. A saddle should be checked once a year by a saddler.

If a crupper is to be used to prevent the saddle from slipping forward, it should be put on when the girths are loose or undone. Standing close to the hind legs, lift up the tail and pass it through the crupper, then draw it up so that it lies under the top of the tail, making sure the hairs are out and lying flat. Attach the crupper to the saddle and adjust the length so that it steadies the saddle without pulling up the tail, as shown in the photograph on the right.

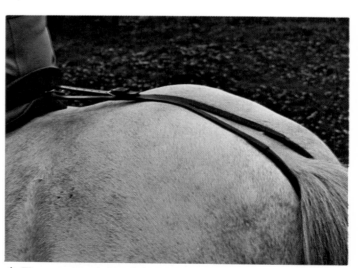

▲ The crupper is used to prevent the saddle from slipping forward and is particularly useful on little ponies. It goes under the pony's tail at one end and attaches at the other to the back D-ring on the saddle. It is correctly adjusted when it holds the saddle firmly without pulling up the tail

Putting on the bridle

The neck strap, an essential aid for the beginner, should be put on before the bridle, either over the horse's neck or fastened round it

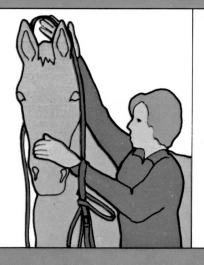

▲ The rider slips the reins over the horse's head and neck, steadying the head with her left hand. The reins should always be put on first so that the rider has something with which to hold and steady the horse if necessary

▲ While the bridle is held in the right hand, the fingers of the left hand feel between the horse's lips where there is a gap between the teeth. This, together with mild pressure, makes the horse open his mouth and the bit can then be gently guided in

▲ Once the bit is in position, the head piece is slipped over each ear in turn. Both hands are needed to carry out this part of the operation and great care is being taken not to hurt the horse's sensitive ears or pull out any of the mane

The bridle should have the throat lash and nose band undone before starting.

First, pass the reins over the horse's head and neck, then slip off the head collar or halter. Take hold of the head piece with your right hand and draw the bridle up the horse's head. With your left hand holding the bit, feel with your fingers between the horse's lips. This, together with gentle pressure, will make the horse open his mouth and the bit can then be guided in. Slide the head piece over each ear in turn, taking care not to pull out any of the mane.

Fasten the throat lash allowing the width of the hand to fit between it and the horse's cheek bone. The throat lash prevents the head piece from slipping over the ears and care must be taken to ensure that it in no way restricts the

◀ The rider has put the bridle on the horse and fastened the throat lash and nose band. By slipping his hand between the throat lash and horse's cheek bone, he has confirmed that it is correctly adjusted

When the throat lash is adjusted correctly, there should be enough room for a hand between it and the horse's cheek bone

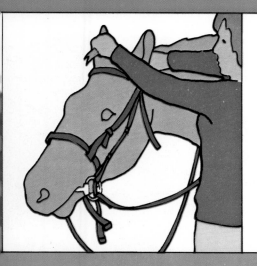

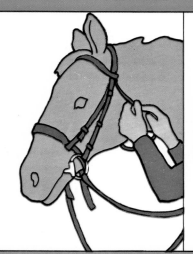

The throat lash has been fastened far too tightly, restricting the horse's breathing and causing him great discomfort

▲ The bridle is now in position. The forelock is being gently eased out from underneath the brow band and the mane from underneath the head piece. The rider should then make sure that none of the pieces is twisted, the brow band is level and the bridle on straight

▲ The throat lash, which prevents the head piece from slipping over the ears, is now being fastened. It should be adjusted to allow a hand's width between it and the horse's cheek bone. If it is any tighter, it will severely restrict the horse's breathing

▲ The nose band is now being fastened. It is in the correct position, lying halfway between the horse's cheek bones and the corners of his mouth, and is comfortably adjusted when two fingers can be inserted between it and the horse's jaw bone

horse's breathing. Then fasten the nose band, allowing approximately two fingers' width between it and the horse's jaw bone, and ensuring that it lies halfway between the cheek bones and the corners of the mouth.

Slip the loose ends of the throat lash and nose band through the keepers (which are like tabs on a belt), then check that the bridle is straight.

If a dropped nose band is being used, the front strap should be positioned well above the nostrils and the back strap fastened behind the jaw, fitting into the horse's chin groove.

The bridle can be put on either before or after the saddle. If it is put on before, your arm should be linked through the reins while you put on the saddle, which will enable you to hold and keep control of the horse.

This horse is tacked up ready for riding, wearing a ▶ snaffle bridle correctly adjusted. The reins are coated with roughened rubber to give the rider extra grip and the rubber stops are for use with a running martingale

First things first
Bridles and saddles

Bridles made of leather are by far the most popular, as they are pliable yet strong and comfortable and, if well cared for, should last indefinitely. They may also be made of braid, rawhide, webbing and nylon. There are three main types of bridle, although these have many variations: the snaffle bridle, the double bridle and the bitless bridle.

The snaffle bridle, two variations of which are shown on the right, is the most widely used of all. It has a single bit which may be any one of the large selection available (see page 106) and a single rein.

The double bridle (illustrated below right) is used for advanced training of the horse or in the show ring. It has two bits: the snaffle bit, called a bridoon in this case, has its own narrow head piece slotted through the brow band beneath the wider main head piece to which the second bit, called a curb, is attached. Both bits have reins.

Another double-reined bridle is that used with the pelham bit (illustrated below right). This has a single head piece but the nature of the bit (see the diagram on page 106) makes it necessary for two reins to be used.

The bitless bridle has no bit but has a special type of nose band, which produces the necessary control by its action on the nose.

The bridle should fit the horse comfortably and allowance be made for lowering or raising of the bit, depending on the type being used. Bridles are designed for many purposes: workman-like and strong for general riding; elegant and neat for the show ring; exotic and decorated for ceremonial occasions.

▼ The bridles, mostly snaffles of one kind or another, are each hung by the head piece, with the reins slipped through the throat lash and the nose band put round the outside. The saddles are all neatly stored on saddle racks

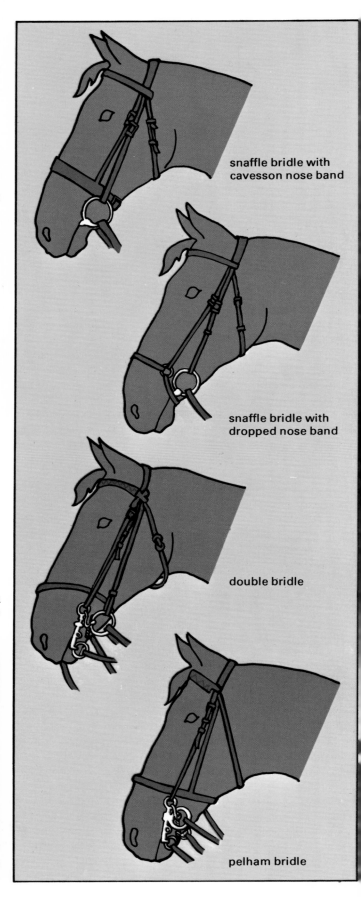

snaffle bridle with cavesson nose band

snaffle bridle with dropped nose band

double bridle

pelham bridle

▲ The three saddles on the fence are from left to right: a general-purpose saddle suitable for riding and jumping; a dressage saddle designed so the rider has a longer leg position for extra impulsion and control; a side-saddle

▼ The racing saddle is very light and is designed so that the jockey can ride very short for balance and extra control. Some racing saddles weigh as little as 680g (1½lb), any extra weight hindering the horse's speed

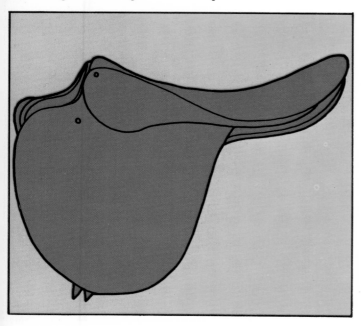

Saddles There are numerous different shapes and sizes of saddle, ranging from general-purpose to dressage, show jumping, racing and side-saddles.

A saddle is an expensive part of the rider's equipment but it never pays to buy a cheap or inferior one. It is often possible to buy a good, second-hand saddle from a saddler who will advise you on the most suitable type.

A general-purpose saddle is the best choice for the everyday rider and to be comfortable it should be shaped so as to assist the rider to sit in the centre and lowest part of the saddle. The weight of the saddle should be evenly distributed on the horse's back and there must be no pressure on the spine or withers.

The frame on which the saddle is built is called a tree, usually made of beechwood, though some are now made of synthetic materials. If the saddle is dropped or rolled on by the horse, the tree may break. A saddle with a broken tree will not only cause serious injury to the horse's back but it loses its value and is expensive to repair.

Ideally, a saddle should be put on a rack, as shown in the photograph opposite, or a saddle horse immediately it is removed from the horse. Cared for in this way, together with yearly tests by a saddler, your saddle will last a lifetime.

First things first
Untacking

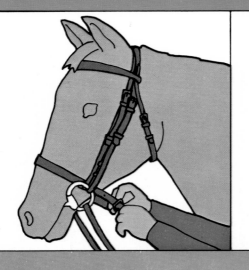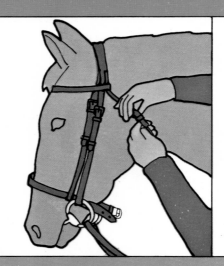

▲ Before starting to untack, the rider should ensure that she has a halter or head collar to hand. The bridle is removed starting from the bottom and working upwards. The nose band is unfastened first

▲ The throat lash is unfastened next. Once this is done, everything is ready and safe for the bridle to be taken off the horse's head

▲ The head piece is gently eased over each of the horse's ears in turn while the reins are held firmly in the right hand to steady the horse and prevent him from moving

▲ At the end of his first ride the rider is now untacking. He has undone the nose band and throat lash and is now gently easing the head piece over the horse's ears, one at a time. The horse's ears are very sensitive, so he is taking great care when carrying out this part of the operation. Always try to untack the horse yourself from the beginning, so that you get to know how it is done

Untacking is fairly easy as, basically, you reverse the tacking-up procedure.

Having dismounted, the first thing you must do is run up your stirrup irons, as shown in the last two diagrams on page 35. These should never be left hanging, as the horse could get his foot caught in them if he kicked out, or they could catch on protruding objects and frighten him.

Before removing the saddle, take the reins off over the horse's head so that you have something with which to hold the horse. Alternatively, slip your left arm through the reins. Raise the saddle flap and unbuckle the girths from the girth straps. Let the girths down gently, taking care that they do not knock the horse's legs.

With one hand on the front arch and the other on the cantle, slide the saddle off towards you and on to your forearm. Take hold of the girths with the other hand as they come over the back and lay them across the seat, just as they were when you started to tack up. Stand the saddle on

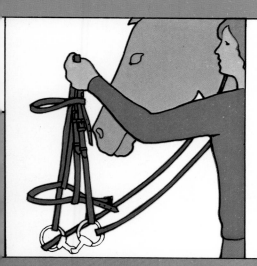

The bit has got caught in the horse's teeth as enough time was not allowed for him to open his mouth when the bridle was lowered

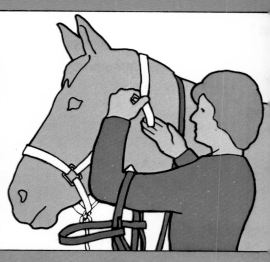

▲ The bridle is now off the horse's head, great care having been taken to release the bit slowly out of his mouth. If the bit is dropped quickly, the horse may throw up his head, get caught in the bit and cause severe injury to his mouth and teeth

▲ Only the reins are left. If the horse is being untacked in his field or stable, the reins can now be slipped over his head and the horse released. The rider holds the head steady with her left hand until this is done

▲ If a halter or head collar is to be put on, this should be done before the reins are removed, so that the rider still has some means of controlling the horse if he moves

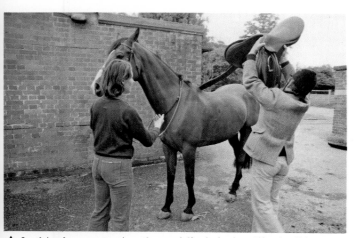

▲ In this demonstration the saddle is being lifted off far too high and the girths are about to fall across the horse's back. The saddle should be slid off the horse's back towards you and on to your left forearm, leaving your right hand free to gather up the girths as they come over the horse's back

a door or gate, or lay it carefully on the ground on its front arch with the girths protecting the pommel and cantle, as shown in the photograph on page 105.

Gently rub the horse's back to restore the circulation and check for any signs of soreness on the back or around the girth.

Before you remove the bridle, put the reins back over the horse's head to ensure you have something with which to control the horse if he moves, and have a head collar or halter to hand. Unfasten the nose band, then the throat lash. Ease the head piece over the ears, then lower the bridle, letting the horse release the bit out of his mouth slowly, so it does not bang on his teeth.

If the horse is to be let loose in his field, remove the reins and release him. If he is to be tied up, put on the head collar or halter before removing the reins.

Your tack should then be picked up and stored ready for cleaning (see page 104).

Riding for pleasure

Hacking – the term used to describe riding for pure pleasure – is one of the most enjoyable pursuits of all, as those who have experienced it will surely confirm. It gives both horse and rider exercise and fresh air, and it is an unrivalled way of seeing the countryside.

Where to ride in urban areas may seem at first to be a problem but even the largest town or city has a wealth of commons, heaths and parks where riders are welcome. Riding in the country is rarely a problem but it is as well to know the sort of terrain you are covering, so that you can recognize such hazards as boggy ground.

In Britain there are still several hundred miles of bridleways and local authorities can give you information on those in your area. In America and Australia riding is well catered for and because of the vast, unpopulated areas of these countries, horses are very much part of the way of life. For this reason long-distance riding has become very popular both in these countries and now in many other parts of the world. Trekking and riding holidays are also popular in many countries and offer enjoyable ways of seeing the countryside and all it has to offer.

If riding in your area is slightly limited in variety, you may like to take advantage of the outings arranged by riding schools. They often organize for groups to visit different parts of the country, so giving the rider the chance to ride new ground and enjoy new scenery.

The photographs show riders enjoying themselves in urban parks, country lanes, on moors, in the mountains and at the seaside.

Get up and go

The first day

Having made your decision to take riding lessons, the first step is to visit a riding school that has been recommended by family or friends or by an official horse society which will have checked it thoroughly to see that it is of a certain standard, has suitable horses and ponies and observes certain safety rules. Although most riding schools are well equipped to cope with beginners, it is always advisable to visit them. On your visit check that the school seems to be well organized, the riders are wearing hard hats, there is a competent adult in charge and that the horses look well cared for. Be very cautious of any school that refuses to show you round.

Once satisfied with the riding school and having booked your lessons, make sure you know the time, duration and price of the lessons and, when the time arrives, that you go suitably clad with sensible shoes and a hard hat, unless you are hiring this from the school, an arrangement which is often possible. During the lesson carry out all instructions given but do not be afraid to question them if you do not understand the reasons.

If you decide to take up riding seriously, it is well worth joining an official horse society which can advise on any aspect of horsemanship. Details of societies are given on page 123. The equestrian magazines on the market are also a useful source of information.

▲ Getting to know your horse is a very important part of the lesson. Always spend a few moments talking to him before you begin and give him a good pat or occasional titbit at the end of the session

The stirrup leathers are being adjusted so that they are ▶ the correct length and comfortable for the rider. This little boy has taken his foot out of the iron, which could be dangerous. If the pony suddenly moved forward the iron could knock against his side and frighten him

▼ The rider has mounted the horse for the first time and, while keeping his feet firmly in the stirrup irons, is being shown how to adjust the leathers. Supervision at all times is essential for every beginner

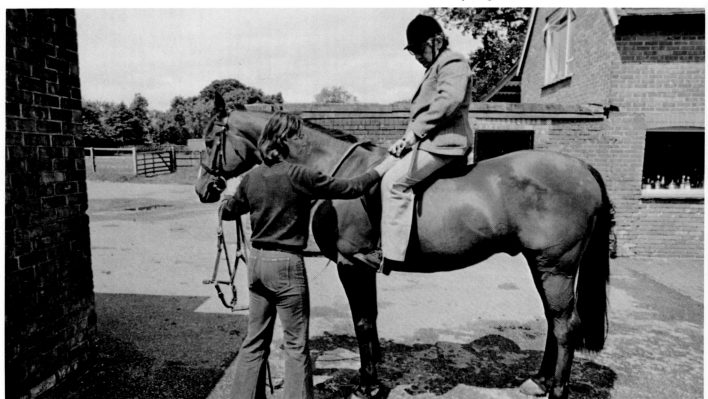

Mounting

Before mounting, the girths should be checked to ensure they are tight enough to hold the saddle firmly in place

The leather is sitting comfortably against the rider's leg, is the correct length and the foot is positioned properly in the stirrup iron

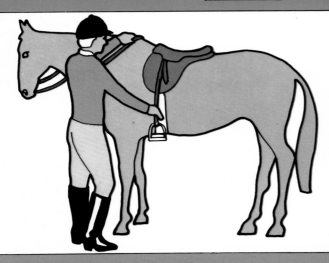

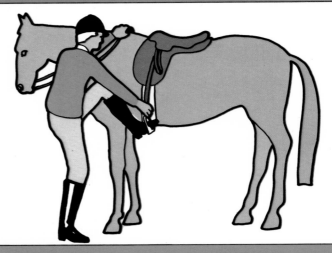

The leather is twisted and will give the rider a sore leg. It is also too long, preventing the heel from being pushed down

▲ The rider is standing at the horse's shoulder. The reins are in his left hand which is placed on the withers just in front of the saddle and he has hold of a piece of mane for anchorage. His right hand is holding the bottom of the stirrup leather and he is swinging the iron outwards and towards him to ensure that he will put his foot into it from the correct side and the leather will not be twisted

▲ Still with a firm hold on the reins and withers, the rider slips his left foot into the stirrup iron while holding it steady with his right hand. He must now swivel round to face the saddle and point his toe well down in the iron so that it will not dig into the horse's ribs as he mounts

Mounting the horse is the first hurdle for the beginner to overcome. Although it is certainly not that easy, once mastered it is the start to so much fun and enjoyment.

The most important thing to remember is that you are dealing with an animal and he has feelings similar to yours. He can experience fear and pain, excitement and tiredness, just as you can and therefore your approach to the horse must be calm and gentle.

Walk towards the horse's nearside shoulder quietly and in an unhurried manner. Never approach him from behind where he cannot see you coming and could kick out in nervousness if he is startled. Talk to him as you approach and put your hand out to stroke his neck.

Having got to know your horse and before attempting to mount, check that your girths are tight enough to hold the saddle firmly and that both stirrup irons are pulled down. The beginner should always have an experienced helper to

hold the horse during this exercise until he feels quite confident of being able to manage unaided.

Face the horse's tail and take the reins in your left hand. Place this hand on the horse's withers just in front of the saddle and take hold of a piece of mane for anchorage. Slip your left foot into the stirrup iron, holding it steady with your right hand. Swivel your body round to face the saddle and point your toe well down in the stirrup iron so that it will not dig into the horse's ribs as you mount. Put your right hand on the seat of the saddle and spring lightly up by pushing down on your left foot. As you straighten your left knee, swing your right leg over the horse's back, taking care not to kick his quarters in the process. At the same time move your right hand to the front arch of the saddle, then allow your body to sink gently into the centre of it. Place your right foot quietly in the stirrup iron, then take hold of the right rein after giving your horse a gentle pat.

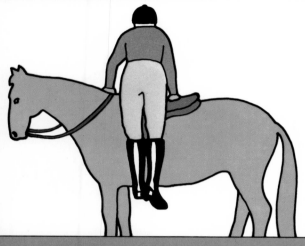

▲ Supporting himself with his right hand on the seat of the saddle, he has sprung up by pushing down on his left foot in the stirrup iron. Now that both legs are straight he can swing his right leg over the horse's back, at the same time moving his right hand from the seat of the saddle to the front arch

▲ With his right hand on the front arch, he lowers himself gently into the centre of the saddle, taking care not to bump down, as this could frighten the horse. He now places his right foot quietly in the stirrup iron which should be turned outwards so that the leather is flat, and takes hold of the reins. He should then make sure he is sitting straight before moving forward

It is essential for the beginner to have a quiet horse on which to practise and so build up his confidence, as it is an exercise which needs time to perfect. But even the quietest horse may sometimes fidget, which is most off-putting for the beginner, so for this reason mounting must always be supervised until the rider is safely on top and confident to walk without help.

For the athletic there are other ways of getting on but until the basics are mastered it is best to stick to the conventional methods.

Vaulting on by grabbing the mane and swinging your body into the air until you can get your legs across the pony's back becomes a necessity for the gymkhana rider. For children it seems remarkably easy and with practice it can be done while the pony is cantering. In case of accidents, however, there should always be two people present and it is an exercise that should not be attempted until the rider is competent at controlling the pony.

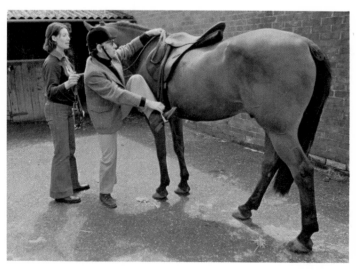

▲ The horse is being held while the beginner mounts. He has hold of the reins and a piece of mane in his left hand and is placing his foot in the stirrup iron, steadying it with his right hand. As this is not an easy exercise for the beginner, it is sensible to use a small horse

Get up and go
Dismounting

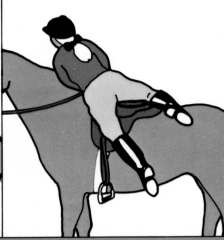

▲ The rider has made sure that the horse is cool and relaxed before she attempts to dismount. With her hands maintaining a light contact on the reins, she slips both feet gently out of the stirrup irons

▲ Taking both reins in her left hand, she places her right hand on the pommel of the saddle and is now in the correct position for dismounting

▲ As she leans forward across the horse's neck, she swings her right leg up and over his back, taking care not to kick his quarters with her foot, and vaults off

Before getting off your horse, make sure that he is cool and preferably dry. If he is not, then walk him around for a few minutes. It is bad horsemanship to dismount from a horse that is hot, sweating and still puffing, so always aim to bring in a cool, dry and relaxed horse.

Sit quietly on the horse and, while maintaining a light contact on the reins, slip both feet out of the stirrup irons. Then take the reins and stick, if you are carrying one, in your left hand. Place your right hand on the pommel of the saddle and lean forward, at the same time swinging your right leg up and over the horse's back. Vault off so that you land on the nearside with your knees bent to take your weight. As with mounting, take great care not to kick the horse's quarters with your foot as you swing your leg over.

Run up your stirrups and take the reins over the horse's head. He is then ready to be led away to his field or stable.

A Continental and Western practice when dismounting is to leave the left foot in the stirrup iron, swing the right leg up and over the horse's quarters, lower the right foot to the ground, then remove the left foot from the iron. This should never be attempted by the beginner, as the slightest movement of the horse will unbalance the rider, with disastrous results, and many accidents have occurred dismounting in this way. It is always wiser to play safe.

For bareback gymkhana events dismounting is done very differently. The rider takes hold of the mane or places the hands either side of the neck and swings the right leg up and over the horse's back, landing with bent knees. Dismounting this way should be practised on both sides. Once you have mastered the art of vaulting off while the pony is standing still, practise it with the pony moving but make sure you have someone leading your pony until you are quite competent.

Another type of dismounting is the unexpected type when you fall off.

The stirrup irons have been run up the under part of the leathers, well out of harm's way

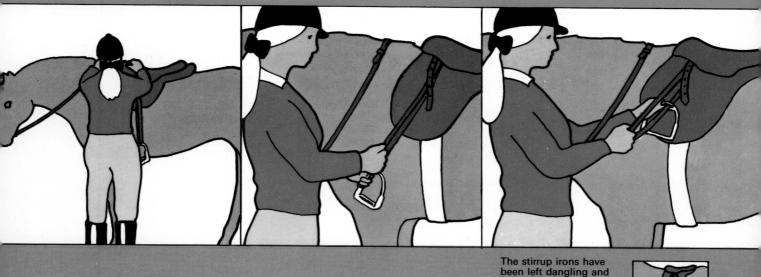

The stirrup irons have been left dangling and will frighten the horse if he moves or bruise him if they knock his elbows and sides

▲ On landing, she makes sure she bends her knees to take her weight, and takes particular care not to pull the reins which could hurt and even injure the horse's mouth

▲ With her left arm through the reins, in order to maintain control of the horse, she takes hold of the stirrup leathers and iron

▲ The stirrup irons are now being run up the under part of the leathers, which can then be slipped back through the irons to ensure they stay securely in place. If the saddle is to be left on for some length of time, the girths should be loosened

If you are about to fall off, the most vital thing to remember is to relax, as in this way you are far less likely to injure yourself. Rolling into a ball and away from the horse is the next stage. This reduces jarring and enables you to get up more quickly and concentrate either on keeping hold of your horse or at least setting off in hot pursuit. Some horses are most understanding and will stand quietly by while you pick up yourself and your self-esteem to have another try!

Never attempt to throw yourself off in panic, as this is asking for a serious accident. Concentrate instead on staying on, keeping calm and working out how best to bring the horse to a stop. Circling or heading for a corner of the field will normally bring a runaway horse to a standstill. You can then dismount in the conventional way.

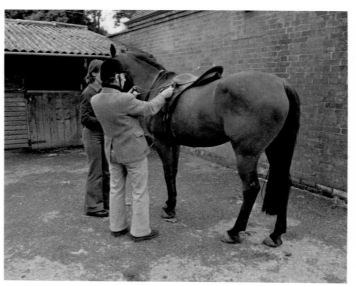

▲ At the end of his lesson the rider has dismounted successfully and is now running the stirrup irons up the under part of the leathers

Position of the rider

Two correct ways of holding the reins: between the little and third fingers then through the hand, or outside the little finger

The correct lower leg position. The leg is resting just on the girth with the heel down and the toe pointing up and forward

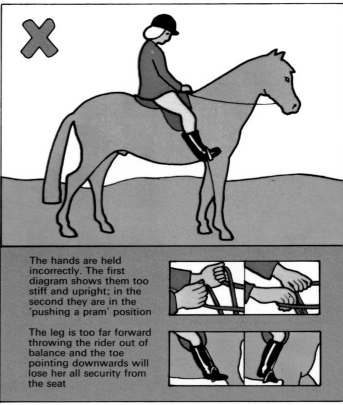

The hands are held incorrectly. The first diagram shows them too stiff and upright; in the second they are in the 'pushing a pram' position

The leg is too far forward throwing the rider out of balance and the toe pointing downwards will lose her all security from the seat

▲ The rider has achieved a good position on the horse. She is sitting square and level, her head and neck carried naturally, her eyes directed between the horse's ears. Her shoulders are relaxed and her arms touching the sides of her body, elbows bent. Her thighs and knees are close against the saddle and her feet are correctly positioned in the irons, heels pushed down and toes pointing forward

▲ The rider is demonstrating a bad riding position. The upper part of the body is slouched, her head is down and her shoulders rounded. Her arms are stiff and she is seated on the back of the saddle, her legs thrown forward and likely to knock the horse's elbow with every stride. The position of her leg has caused her foot to slide too far through the iron and her toes to point upwards

The position of the rider on the horse should look as natural as possible and he should aim to appear to be part of the horse rather than perched on top. There should be no feeling of stiffness, for if one part of the body is tense, it will affect the others.

The upper part of the body should be in the natural seated position, square and level, with the head and neck carried naturally erect and facing forward. The eyes should be directed between the horse's ears. Overall, the body should appear straight but not stiff, relaxed but not slack.

The arms should hang loosely from the shoulders, elbows bent and touching the sides of the body. The forearms and wrists, which, viewed from the side, should be in a straight line through the reins to the horse's mouth, must remain supple so that they can act as a buffer between the rider and the horse's mouth.

The hands should be carried slightly apart

from and just above either side of the horse's withers. The backs of the hands should face outwards with the thumbs uppermost resting lightly on the reins. The wrists must be supple and not rounded. When riding, the hands must be very sensitive, ready to follow the horse's every movement, drawing slightly back to control and balance the horse, then releasing again as the horse responds. It is most important not to cross the reins over the withers when steering, as this confuses the horse who no longer has a direct feel on one side of his mouth.

If the seat and lower part of the body is wrongly positioned, it will throw the rest of the body into a bad position. The rider should be seated well down in the centre and lowest part of the saddle and not look as if he has been stuck on top. It is this depth into the saddle which makes riding so much easier.

The upper part of the leg should stretch well down from the hip with the thigh lying flat

against the saddle. The knee should be rolled on to the saddle and never allowed to roll outwards. The grip of the thigh and knee should be downward and inward.

The lower part of the leg should rest just behind the girth and is in the correct position when the rider can see the tip of his toes below his knee. The leg should hang lightly touching the horse's side, with the stirrup leather vertical to the ground. The leg must be free to use on the horse when necessary. At no time should the calf grip the saddle, as this would cause the heel to lift and so lose the security of the correct leg position and put the rider out of balance.

The feet should always be placed right home in the stirrup irons while learning to ride, the heel pushed downwards with the toes resting through the irons and facing forward in a natural position. Toes turned in or out will affect the position of the legs and cause stiffness in the ankles. Later, as the rider becomes more experienced and has a good, firm seat, he can practise riding with the iron on the ball of the foot. The weight should be on the inside of the iron and this will help the rider to bring his knee and thigh closer to the saddle. When jumping, the foot should be right home for security.

A simple rule to follow when trying to achieve the correct position in the saddle is to grow taller

▲ The rider is in a good position on her horse, her body straight but not stiff, relaxed but not slack. Her overall appearance is one of neatness and confidence, and being part of the horse rather than simply perched on top

from the seat upwards and grow longer from the seat downwards.

Bad habits form easily, so make certain you avoid the following: head poked forward, rounded shoulders which make the upper arms stick out in a most unattractive fashion, stiff arms, rigid hands, a slouching back or one that is too stiff. Avoid leaning too far forward or too far back and make sure your legs are not too far forward or back with the toes down and the heel up. Do not let your knees hang off the saddle and your heels grip the poor, unfortunate horse. He will move forward only to be caught in the teeth as you lose your balance!

In striving to achieve the correct riding position, remember to keep your head up, looking ahead between the horse's ears, your shoulders relaxed but back, your arms close to the body with bent elbows and supple hands. Sit well down in the saddle, your back straight and legs hanging naturally, with thighs and knees close to the saddle, heels down and toes pointed forward. Above all, remember that you must feel comfortable and secure before moving forward.

Steering and control

The rider is steering to the right yet has remained sitting quite straight. Leaning in or out puts extra strain on the horse

The rider is in a good position. Her hands are nicely placed by the withers where they should remain for all ground work

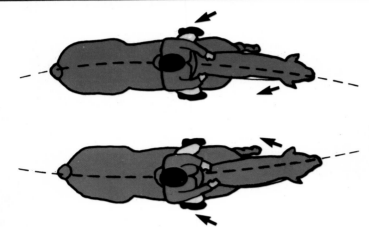

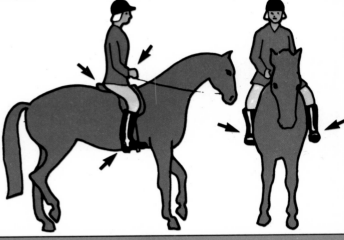

Leaning as the horse rounds a corner is a bad habit. The rider's extra weight on one side makes it difficult for the horse to maintain his balance

The hands have come up, pulling the head awkwardly. They should be kept low so the bit acts correctly in the horse's mouth

The diagrams show which aids are used to instruct the horse to turn, slow down in pace and halt, and how those aids are used. To turn the horse to the right, the right rein is pulled gently but firmly and pressure applied with the left leg to push the horse round. To turn the horse to the left, the left rein and right leg are used. To ask the horse to slow down in pace or halt, pressure is applied with the seat and legs while the hands firmly pull the reins, bunching the horse together so he slows down. If the horse has a hard mouth owing to bad schooling, more pulling on the reins and less leg pressure may be needed for this exercise. The hands should be kept down and the reins never pulled harder than necessary. Once the horse has obeyed the instruction, the hold should be relaxed

When learning how to control the horse, it is important to remember that you are dealing with an animal and one that in its natural state roams about at will. When the horse is ridden by man he has a hard lesson to learn; he can no longer do as he wishes but must now obey his master.

Through the ages the horse has been the friend of man, serving him in many ways and during this time man has acquired a greater knowledge of the horse than of any other animal.

To convey your wishes to the horse, it is important that they are clearly asked for and easily understood. Some horses are obviously quicker to understand and happier to please than others but you must always ask and never force your demands on a horse if you are to achieve a willing response.

Steering and controlling the horse are carried out by means of aids, signals with which instructions are conveyed to the horse. There are two kinds of aid: natural and artificial.

The natural aids are the hands, the body, the legs and the voice. Artificial aids are whips or sticks, spurs and martingales. Spurs are unsuitable for the beginner and martingales should be used only under supervision. The use of the stick is discussed on page 54.

The rider's hands direct the horse, help to regulate the pace and, combined with the body and legs, control the impulsion. The hands must always be very gentle, sensitive and quick to act. There should always be a light contact with the horse's mouth, except when relaxing on a loose rein. The hands control the front end of the horse, they guide, control and alter his balance by moving his head up, down or to the side.

Some horses have hard mouths, caused by bad riding over a period of time or from incorrect schooling. In such cases, steering and controlling the horse is a problem, as it is difficult for an inexperienced rider to maintain a light contact when the horse is unresponsive.

▲ As mother and son turn their horses in opposite directions, it is clear to see how each is applying pressure on the horse's side with the outside leg behind the girth, while steering his head by pulling firmly on the inside rein

The body, depending on its position, can create impulsion and reduce or increase the pace. By leaning forward slightly, for instance when jumping, the weight comes off the quarters so that the horse's legs can be used to the maximum in the take-off over the fence. On landing, the weight of the body comes back into the saddle, thus freeing the front and making it easier for the horse to pick himself up after the fence. As the rider advances and becomes more experienced, so the use of the body comes more into action as more control is required.

The back muscles play an important part. When relaxed they enable the rider to maintain good balance and security in the seat; when braced they influence the horse in conjunction with the corresponding hand and leg aids.

The legs control the quarters and help to balance the horse. By pressing the legs against the horse's sides, pace or energy can be increased. The more pressure the rider uses with his legs, the lighter the front of the horse becomes and this pressure, combined with control by the hands, has the effect of bunching the horse together. By using the legs separately it is possible to guide the quarters one way or another. When riding in circles it is often necessary to apply more pressure with your outside leg to control the quarters and prevent them from swinging out.

The voice is extremely important, as it assists the rider to calm, encourage and control the horse. It is particularly useful in the training of young horses and when lunging (see page 72), which can be done completely at the word of command.

Used together, the aids make it possible to control and balance the horse so that he, in turn, has the maximum control over his limbs.

With guidance, the beginner will soon discover for himself how, by combining the use of legs, hands and body, the horse can be made to shorten or lengthen his stride, to stop, start and turn with relative ease.

The walk and halt

The rider is sitting upright and relaxed, his hands in the correct position on the withers, maintaining a light contact on the reins

As the horse has moved forward, the rider has lost his balance. His body has shot backwards, causing his hands to come up

▲ The walk is a pace of four-time, the horse lifting each leg independently as he moves forward. The rider is in the basic riding position and to make the horse move forward he has eased the reins slightly and applied gentle pressure with his legs against the horse's sides just behind the girths. Once on the move, the rider relaxes his legs and maintains a light contact on the horse's mouth

▲ The first leg to be picked up is the near-hind leg, as shown in the first diagram, followed by the near-fore as shown above. The rider is sitting relaxed and upright, his body moving in rhythm with the natural movement of the horse and he is maintaining a light contact on the reins, his hands placed close together just above the withers

The walk, being the slowest pace, is obviously the easiest one to master. It also enables the rider to practise turning, steering and quickly to gain confidence and a feeling of achievement.

To make the horse walk forward, you should remain in the basic riding position but slightly ease the reins and apply gentle pressure with the legs against the horse's sides just behind the girths. As soon as the horse moves forward, the lower leg should be relaxed and a light contact maintained on the horse's mouth. If the horse slows down, more leg pressure is required; if he goes too fast, ease the leg pressure and apply a little more contact on the reins.

The lower leg helps to balance the horse and to guide the quarters. It is important to remember to keep the knees close to the saddle and the legs hanging in a natural position without clinging with the heels. Practise walking slowly, remembering to keep the heels down all the time. Then practise walking freely, holding the reins loosely and so allowing the horse complete freedom of his head and neck.

To halt, squeeze gently with both legs behind the girths, ease the weight of your body very slightly back and apply a firmer pressure on the reins. As soon as the horse halts, loosen the reins and sit quite still. This helps the horse to relax and remain motionless.

If the horse halts with his head up in the air, this indicates that you have been too hard on the reins or have not used quite enough leg pressure to help him balance himself as he slowed down. Practise walking and halting until you feel quite happy that you are under control, before attempting the next pace.

Walking unaided for the first time, this rider is coping ▶ well. As his confidence increases, he will be able to sit with his back a little straighter and adopt a stronger leg position by pushing his heel further down, so bringing the lower leg slightly further back just behind the girths

▲ The off-hind leg is now being picked up and there is no change in the rider's position. His position should remain the same throughout this exercise. Sadly, not all horses will answer the rider's aids promptly and willingly. Bad schooling may have hardened their mouths and in some cases a firm kick with the legs and heels may be the only effective way of getting a response

▲ The last leg to be picked up is the off-fore and this completes the sequence of the walk. At the end of the exercise the rider should bring the horse to a halt by squeezing gently with both legs behind the girths, easing the weight of the body very slightly back and applying a firmer pressure on the reins. As soon as the horse halts, the rider should loosen the reins and sit quite still

The trot

The rider has the reins too long and will not be able to control the horse. Her body is leaning forward and out of balance

▲ The trot is a pace of two-time, the horse springing from one pair of diagonals to the other. In the first movement the off-hind leg and near-fore are off the ground, while the other two take all the weight. The rider demonstrating the rising trot has been thrust very slightly forward and upwards as the horse moves and starts to change on to the other diagonal. Now she is out of the saddle, her body is straight

▲ The off-hind and near-fore are now moving forward and extending before coming to the ground. The rider has come down into the saddle and sits as the horse changes on to the opposite diagonal. She is seated upright and relaxed, well in the saddle, with the small of her back supple. Her legs are in the correct position – they must not be allowed to slide forwards or backwards as she rises

The trot is a pace of two-time in which there is a moment of suspension when all four feet are off the ground. It is an alternate movement of two diagonals, the right diagonal being the off-fore leg and the near-hind, the left diagonal being the near-fore and the off-hind. It can be ridden either rising or sitting.

In the rising or posting trot, the rider sits for one bump and rises for the next as the horse moves forward changing from one diagonal to the other. To ask the horse to trot, use the same aids as for the walk. Apply pressure to the horse's sides with the legs, brace the seat muscles and urge the horse forward, easing both reins slightly. Wait until the horse, by its increased impulsion, throws you up in the saddle, then keep rising up and down smoothly to the rhythm of the horse, keeping an even, light contact on the reins. You should not have to force yourself to rise in the saddle; your body should be in such a position that it is thrown up

naturally. If the horse slows down, a little more leg pressure is required; if he goes too fast, relax the leg pressure and shorten your reins.

It is important to maintain the correct basic riding position and not to lean back at any stage, which will cause you to lose your balance. Your body should remain upright and supple, leaning slightly forward as you rise in the saddle. If at any stage you feel you are losing your balance, take hold of the neck strap or a piece of mane, always easing yourself forward rather than back.

At the sitting trot the rider remains sitting throughout, allowing his back to give with the movement of the horse. This teaches the rider to sit deep in the saddle, so essential to success.

This experienced rider schooling her horse is ▶ demonstrating the collected trot. The steps are shorter than those of the ordinary trot and the horse is lighter and more mobile. She is sitting deep in the saddle and is producing the elevation of the horse's legs by the correctly combined use of the seat muscles, legs and hands

The lower leg stays in the same position throughout the trot, the weight of the body when rising being taken on the knee

The rider's position is upright the whole time, her weight being put very slightly forward only as she rises out of the saddle

The leg has shot forward because the rider is either sitting too far back in the saddle or is leaning back, out of balance

The rider is leaning back, her hands have come up and she is pulling the reins in an effort to retrieve her balance

▲ The opposite diagonal is now coming into action, the near-hind and off-fore being picked up. The rider has risen out of the saddle once again, her body supported through her knee joints. While she is rising up and down in the saddle her hands must remain still and in the same position, just above the withers. Any movement or change in position will upset and unbalance the horse

▲ The near-hind and off-fore are now moving forward and extending before coming to the ground, completing the sequence as the rider sits again in the saddle. The four pictures demonstrate a nice, free trot, with the rider maintaining the correct body position and a light contact on the reins throughout

Get up and go
The canter

▲ The canter is a pace of three-time in which the horse propels himself forward in three stages followed by a moment of suspension when all four feet are off the ground. In the first movement the off-hind leg is taking all the weight while the other three legs are in the air, about to move forward. The rider is sitting correctly, well down in the saddle, maintaining the pace by pressure from the legs

▲ The next stage shows the off-fore and near-hind legs on the ground. The rider is allowing his body to follow the rhythm and movement of the horse without any noticeable change in position taking place, his back remaining supple and relaxed throughout. His legs remain on the girths and his hands, placed together just above the withers, hold the reins lightly but firmly

The canter is a pace of three-time which means there are three beats to each stride. The rider should sit upright, still and well down in the saddle. His back should be supple and relaxed so that he does not bump in the saddle but follows the rhythm and movement of the horse.

To ask the horse to canter from trot, you must stop rising and sit in the saddle. Take a firmer hold of the reins, so that the horse does not go at a faster trot, then squeeze the horse's sides with your legs behind the girths to push him from a slow trot into a steady, slow canter. When he is cantering, ease the reins slightly and maintain the pace by pressure from the legs. If the horse goes too fast, relax the leg pressure slightly and shorten the reins, keeping the hands low by the withers.

If at any stage the horse feels out of control, pull him round in a circle, large enough so that he cannot slip over but small enough to slow him

down. The worst thing you can do is panic. This will result in your clinging more tightly with your legs, thus indicating to the confused horse a wish to go faster!

As you progress you will realize that, by indicating the instruction clearly to the horse, you will be able to ask him to strike off into canter on the right or left diagonal, according to the direction in which you wish to go. To canter to the right, you should take a slightly firmer feel of the right rein and push the horse into canter with both legs, the left leg positioned slightly further back to act as a balance to control the quarters. To canter to the left, follow the same procedure but use the left rein and the right leg. Practise just a few strides at a time when you first start cantering until you are quite confident.

The rider is using plenty of determination to keep his somewhat reluctant pony cantering. He is doing well, despite the fact that he is leaning slightly too far forward in an effort to achieve greater impulsion ▶

The rider is seated well down in the saddle, his back giving to absorb the horse's movement, his hands placed just above the withers

A stiff and rigid back causes the rider to bounce up and down in the saddle and jar his spine with the horse's every stride

▲ At this stage the off-hind has left the ground and is about to come forward to start another propelling movement. The weight is now on the right diagonal with the near-fore stretched forward ready to make the third beat of the stride

▲ All four feet are now off the ground. The fore legs are about to come up as the off-hind meets the ground to start the sequence again. Throughout the canter the rider must be upright, as any leaning of the body will unbalance the horse. He must not allow himself to round his back or shoulders, his elbows should be kept close to the body and the toes must remain facing forward

The gallop

The rider is perched slightly forward over her hands, taking the weight out of the saddle and on to her legs

The reins are too long causing the rider to lose control and shoot back as the horse moves

▲ The gallop is a fast canter but because of the increased speed it becomes a four-time pace as the horse does not put the diagonals down together. Instead, the four legs follow one another independently. In the first movement all the weight is on the near-fore and the off-fore is stretched forward. The hind legs are extended before coming through to push the horse up and onwards

▲ The near-hind has come to the ground closely followed by the off-hind and is taking the weight as the fore legs come up and start to extend. The rider is perched slightly forward over her hands, her weight being taken out of the saddle and on to her legs, while she balances herself with her knees. Her hands are steady, holding the reins firmly and resting on the horse's neck

The gallop is the fastest pace. It is similar to the canter but because of the increased speed it becomes a four-time pace in which the horse's four legs follow one another independently.

At the gallop the rider should stand up slightly in the stirrup irons and lean forward, taking the weight off the seat. He should shorten the reins and keep his hands low on the withers. His legs should remain in the normal position and it is essential that they do not become rigid and stiff, for they should act as shock absorbers, taking the weight of the body. It is usually advisable to shorten the stirrup leathers a couple of holes before galloping, as they feel rather long when you are standing up in the irons. Galloping should not be attempted until the rider is fully competent at the other paces and can easily stop the horse.

To ask the horse to gallop, first ask him to canter. Then, sitting well down in the saddle, urge him forward with your seat and legs,

keeping a firm hold of the reins. It is important not to pull at the horse with reins that are too long, as this will only excite him and make him go faster.

To stop a galloping horse, ease the pressure from your legs, sit a little more upright in the saddle and take a firm pull on the reins, squeezing very gently with the legs to balance the quarters. If the horse is difficult to stop, pull him round in a circle or into the corner of a field.

Fun as it is to gallop, it is a pace that can excite a horse if done in excess and care should be taken not to gallop too often or in the same area, as the horse will then become used to galloping there and it will be difficult for the rider to dissuade him. Do not gallop an unfit horse.

The rider is well in control of his horse at the gallop, ▶ standing up slightly in his stirrups and leaning forward. Because he is riding at speed, he has shortened the reins so his hands are either side of the horse's neck. The whole weight of the horse is on the off-fore leg

The rider's hands holding the reins are positioned far too high above the horse's neck, pulling the head up awkwardly

▲ The off-fore is stretched out and about to take the weight as the momentum of speed carries the horse on and the other legs off the ground. The rider is keeping a steady feel on the reins and sitting quite still, so essential in maintaining the horse's balance at this pace

▲ The horse's whole weight is now transferred on to the off-fore. The other three legs are airborne and are coming through to start another stride. It is virtually impossible to be able to see naturally what happens as a horse gallops. One of the only ways is by watching slow-motion films, the best examples of which are often shown on the television sports programmes

On with the show

The three most hotly contested competitions in equestrian sport are dressage, show jumping and eventing. These are Olympic events and in between the Games there are regional games such as the European Championships, the Pan American Games and the World Championships.

Dressage is the art of high-school training of the horse, demanding the ultimate in work on the flat. The highest test is the Grand Prix for which the horse is required to do such movements as Passage, Piaffe, Pirouettes and Flying Changes.

Show jumping is the test of the horse's jumping capabilities, the winner being the horse with the fewest faults over a course of obstacles.

Eventing is the complete all-round training of the horse, consisting of dressage, cross country and show jumping phases. The ultimate is the Three-Day Event in which the second day, consisting of a 24-kilometre (15-mile) course including a steeplechase phase, roads and tracks, and cross country section, is the most influential.

▲ Paul Schockemöhle on Talisman
▼ Alwin Schockemöhle on Santa Monica

▼ Harvey Smith on Graffiti

▲ Ann Moore on Psalm

▲ Jeff McVean on Blue Gift

▲ Bill Steinkraus on Mainspring

Thanks to television, some of the world's top equestrian sportsmen and women have become household names. These and the following pages show well-known horses and riders from the show jumping, eventing and dressage worlds.

Some famous show jumping horses are Boomerang, Philco, Moxy, Pennwood Forge Mill, St James, Towerlands Anglezark, Sanyo Sanmar, Ryan's Son, Sportsman, Everest For Ever, and Mr Roth.

Germany has had two highly talented riders in Gerd

continued on next page

▲ Colonel Piero d'Inzeo on Easter Light
◀ Chris Boylen on Jungherr

Wiltfang, for many years the World Champion, and Alwin Schockemöhle, who in 1976 won the Olympic Show Jumping Gold Medal with the only double clear round. His brother Paul also ranks among Germany's most successful rider

Consistently successful British riders have included David Broome, World Champion in 1970, the indomitable Harvey Smith, his son Robert Smith, Caroline Bradley, Paddy McMahon, Nick Skelton and Derek Ricketts. Australians John Fahey and Kevin Bacon and Canadians Jim Day and James Elder have all done exceptionally well in Europe and America. Ireland's stylish Eddie Macken, James Kernan and Paul Darragh, Americans Melanie Smith and Michael Mats, Austria's Hugo Simon and Italy's d'Inzeo brothers have thrilled show jumping crowds everywhere with their superb horsemanship.

The dressage world has been dominated by the great Granat, with strong competition from Slibowitz, Mon Chéri, Ahlerich and Hirtentraum.

Well-known riders in the eventing world include Britons Richard Meade, Lucinda Prior-Palmer, HRH The Princess Anne and Captain Mark Phillips.

▲ Marion Mould on Elizabeth Ann

▲ HRH The Princess Anne on Doublet

▲ Caroline Bradley on True Lass

▲ Captain Mark Phillips on Columbus

▲ David Broome on Sportsman

▲ Paddy McMahon on Streamline

▲ Richard Meade on Jacob Jones

Tips and advice   How to progress

▲ Going out for rides – especially in a group – is not only a relaxing pastime but increases the rider's knowledge of his horse and his confidence. The members of the group can learn a great deal by watching each other as they ride and spotting the common faults

The rider is allowing the horse to have a bite of grass. He has kept a firm hold on the reins, but may not have enough control if the horse moves off suddenly. It is advisable to dismount and hold the reins to let the horse eat ▶

Having become fairly confident and competent at increasing and decreasing the pace, you must now concentrate on your position while carrying out these exercises. To avoid falling into bad habits – something which is so easy to do – you must work hard from the beginning at achieving the correct position at all times, for this is the basis of successful riding.

Ensure that you have a firm seat in the saddle and a good leg position, pushing the heel well down without tightening the leg muscles and keeping the toe slightly up and pointing straight ahead all the time. Are your arms positioned correctly? They should hang close to the body, bent at the elbows with the wrists and hands nicely supple, ready to give and take the reins as necessary.

Do not forget to talk to your horse. The voice has a very calming effect on him when used quietly but shouting and screaming will only frighten and bewilder him. Many horses are trained to obey the voice which helps to make the change of pace easy to achieve.

It is important to be able to change direction,

so practise changing the rein, riding circles and figures of eight, and riding into corners rather than cutting across them. As you progress, accuracy will become an increasingly important aspect, so you must be able to make your horse go exactly where you want him to, when you want him to. He must be made to halt, walk, trot and canter at your demand, all of which takes time and a great deal of practice to achieve.

Going out for rides is not only a relaxing pastime but it is a useful way for you to increase your confidence. It also gives you the chance to gain more awareness of your horse and develop a light and sympathetic contact on the reins. The best riders learn to feel how a horse is going to react to each situation and to ride him accordingly. If the horse is tense and excitable, it is vital that you relax totally and calm him by gentle talking and stroking. A lazy horse may need to be pushed on quite firmly and even given a tap with a stick to remind him there is work to do. As you gain experience, you will quickly be able to gauge the sort of horse you are on and to react accordingly.

Use of a stick

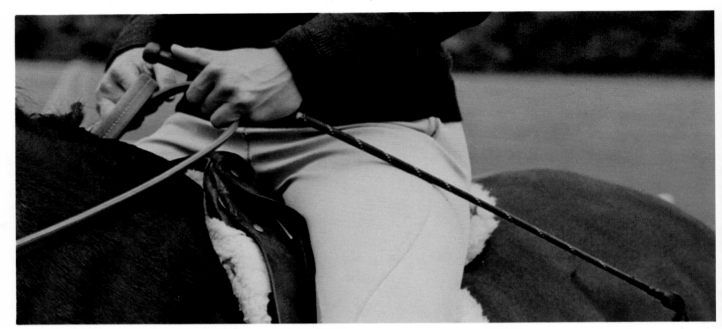

The stick or whip is a useful aid for correction and creating extra impulsion. It is carried with the thumb uppermost and when it is put into use, the hand should be taken off the rein, to prevent pulling on the horse's mouth, and returned immediately afterwards. The photographs above and below clearly demonstrate this exercise.

It is important to become proficient at using the stick in either hand and at exactly the moment it is needed, so that the horse understands at once why he is being corrected. It should never be used harshly or unnecessarily and it is better to give one firm hit than a lot of irritating taps.

The most commonly used, all-purpose variety is the short cutting whip which has a broad, leather, flap end and a rounded top. The show cane, usually plain or leather-covered, is carried at its balancing point and used in the show ring. The hunting crop, also held at its balancing point but with the hook to the rear pointing downwards, should always have a thong and lash attached. The hook is used for opening, holding and closing gates.

A perfectly adequate stick to use in the early stages of riding is a hazel stick from the hedgerow, provided any prominent branches or buds are removed before it is put into use.

Opening a gate

Opening a gate while seated on a horse may seem to be a daunting prospect but it is really extremely simple. As long as the latch is easy to operate, you will be able to open a gate while sitting on a horse as easily as you can while standing on firm ground! Ride towards the hinges of the gate, then turn the horse in the direction of the latch, so that he is standing parallel and close to the gate. Transfer the reins and stick to the hand furthest away from the gate, so leaving your other hand free. Now lean forward and unfasten the latch.

Pull the gate towards you, reining back your horse as you do so. Most horses will automatically go back a few steps as you pull open the gate, before walking round and through. Obviously this exercise is much easier if you are riding a well schooled horse familiar with the procedure of opening gates. If at this stage you are getting into difficulties and there is no one to help, rather than frighten or worry the horse it is better to dismount, run up your stirrup irons so that they do not catch on the gate-hooks and lead him through.

Having guided your horse gently through the gate, turn him round. Transfer the reins and stick to the hand furthest from the gate, so leaving the other hand free to pull the gate towards you, reining back the horse as you do so. The horse demonstrating this exercise is a well schooled, quiet veteran who knows exactly what he is doing. However, if the horse you are riding is young and somewhat unpredictable, it is advisable to dismount. The cattle grid beside the gate could prove to be a dangerous hazard and you could risk an accident if he stepped on it.

Pull the gate to, then turn the horse in the direction of the latch, so that he is standing parallel and close to the gate. With your hand nearest the gate still free, the other one holding the reins and stick, lean forward and fasten the latch. Always make your horse stand still while you are opening and closing gates, so that he will learn the procedure and so stand quietly when you have a difficult gate to open. If the gate is narrow, place your leg well forward on the horse's shoulder, to avoid catching it on the posts or gate-hooks. A hunting crop is particularly useful in helping to open and shut gates.

Tips and advice
Coping with problems

At some stage during your riding career you will inevitably come up against problems.

You will discover the most common of all probably during your first riding lesson. Your instructor and the books will tell you to squeeze with the legs and the horse will move forward. Unless you are lucky and are riding a well schooled horse, it is more than likely that you will eventually have to give some good, hard kicks before getting a response. Likewise, a gentle pull on the reins will invariably become quite a hard tug before the horse will stop.

Although this is not too worrying, it does in fact set the beginner off badly in that he will think from the start that all horses need kicks and pulls to induce the required result. It is therefore important to let the beginner know whether he is dealing with a well schooled horse or one that has a hard mouth and is unresponsive to the leg.

Most problems can be dealt with if a little common sense is used. Patience with animals is essential and you should never lose your temper however infuriating a time you are having.

Perhaps the first thing to consider is the reason for the problem. Does the horse appear frightened? Is he not sufficiently well trained to be able to cope with your request? Maybe he does not understand what is being expected of him or he is simply being naughty. The reason must be found and then dealt with accordingly. Something may have happened to the horse before you came to ride him and this experience may be the key to his bad behaviour.

Most problems in the stable can be sorted out with patient and sensible handling. Never allow the horse the opportunity to be difficult or vicious, and be sensitive to his moods, so that he is not annoyed by over-vigorous grooming, or teased unnecessarily, even if unconsciously, by being kept waiting for a feed. Such things can make a big difference to stable manners.

Horses that are difficult to catch present real problems. If you know your horse is a problem, put him in a small paddock and always with a head collar so that at least you have something to take hold of. Take a bowl of food with you and do not grab at the horse as you approach. Let him eat some of the food before quietly attempting to take hold of him. If there are others to help, try slowly to get the horse into a corner but never chase after him if he gets away.

Loading a horse into a trailer or horsebox can sometimes be a problem. If patience and a bowl of food do not work, enlist the help of two assistants to hold a long rein or rope behind and

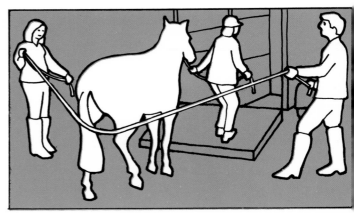

▲ If you cannot load your horse into a horsebox or trailer by means of patience and a bowl of food, you may need the help of two assistants to hold a long rein or rope behind and below the horse's quarters and pull it firmly and continuously while you lead the horse quietly in

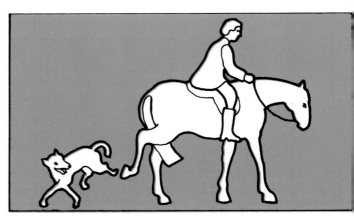

▲ A kicking horse is a danger. While you are riding you are responsible for your horse's actions, so make sure you turn him towards his likely victim. Warn people to keep clear of his quarters, turn his head inwards towards hounds when out hunting and keep away from crowded areas

▲ When you are riding a horse that pulls, make sure your reins are sufficiently short for you to keep control and so prevent him from taking off. Horses pull for a variety of reasons and in some cases the only solution may be to use a stronger bit

below the horse's quarters and give it a firm, continuous pull, while you lead the horse in. Alternatively, get them to lock their hands behind and below the horse's quarters and exert a firm pull. A difficult loader will often go into the trailer or horsebox quite happily if another horse is already loaded.

Kickers are a menace and in this case prevention is the best solution. Always turn the horse's quarters away from the person or thing he is likely to kick. Tell people to keep clear and if your horse tries to kick, give him a good ticking off immediately. Out hunting, a red ribbon on the horse's tail denotes a kicker. Always turn your horse's head inwards towards hounds or dogs to avoid kicking them.

Pullers can be frightening and again it is essential to discover and deal with the reason for the behaviour. It may be excitability, fright, overfeeding, an uncomfortable bit or bad hands of the rider. There is a lot of truth in the saying 'If you don't pull at him, he won't pull at you', and so often this in itself works. When you are riding a puller, always make sure your reins are sufficiently short for you to keep control from the start and try to avoid letting the horse reach the stage when control is lost. In some cases a stronger bit may be required but this should be used only if the rider has good, sympathetic hands.

Rearing is an unpleasant experience for the rider. It may be the horse's way of rebelling against discipline or it may be caused by some frightening experience the horse has suffered in the past. It is important to be able to feel whether your horse is frightened or simply being disobedient. The frightened horse may need reassurance yet firmness but above all patience; the disobedient horse needs a firm approach and discipline. Turning the horse in a small circle as he attempts to rear sometimes helps and riding firmly forward is important at all times.

Refusals when jumping are usually caused by the fence being too high or the rider approaching it incorrectly. If the fence is too high, lower it and jump it when small, then gradually build up the height again. If you have approached the fence incorrectly, take your horse back and try again, this time ensuring you give more room on your approach. Never let your horse refuse and run out to the side. He must not be allowed to get into bad habits and, so long as he is capable of negotiating the fence, you should coax him onwards with quiet insistence.

▲ A horse rearing is an unpleasant experience for the rider. If he rears because he does not want to go forward, patience and determination are needed to coax him on. Sit well forward on the rearing horse and hang on to the mane rather than the bit, in case this pulls him over backwards

▲ Refusals when jumping are usually caused by the fence being too high or the rider approaching it incorrectly. Consider the reason, then correct the mistake either by lowering the fence, then building it up again gradually, or by giving more room on your approach

Jump for joy   Introduction to jumping

▲ Trotting over poles is the first exercise in jumping for the beginner to practise. The poles should be approximately 1-1·50m (3-4ft) apart and the horse should maintain a good rhythm while trotting over them. He is unlikely to jump them but he will elevate his stride over them and the rider will get to know the feel of the horse, the reaction to the poles and so increase his confidence

Once you have become fairly confident on the flat, you will naturally want to move on to the next stage, which is jumping.

Never attempt at the beginning to do more than you feel confident of achieving. The first stages of jumping are so important, for once you can jump small fences happily, the bigger ones are only a matter of time, practice and confidence.

The beginner should have a horse that knows his job and will jump safely and smoothly over whatever he attempts. The most important thing for the rider to remember when jumping is to stay forward over the fence and avoid pulling the horse in the mouth. For this reason, he should be encouraged to hold on to the neck strap or a piece of mane to maintain his balance.

First, consider the position of the horse on the approach, take-off, period of suspension and landing. As the horse approaches the fence he lowers his head and stretches his neck, allowing himself to balance and prepare for the jump. On take-off he shortens his neck and lifts up his fore legs. As he brings his hind legs under him, he stretches his head and neck and springs upwards and forward. During the period of suspension his head and neck are stretched full out, slightly downwards. The hind legs are brought up underneath him. As he lands, his head comes up and his neck shortens.

The first exercise to practise is trotting over poles laid on the ground. Practise on one to

begin with, then add a few more, placing them approximately 1-1·50m (3-4ft) apart. Although the horse is unlikely to jump them, he will elevate his stride over them and the rider will experience the feel of the horse, learn how he reacts to the poles and so gain confidence.

The next stage is for the beginner to practise the jumping position which is described on the following two pages. For the moment trot for a few strides while standing up in the stirrup irons and leaning slightly forward, then relax. This exercise should be practised several times before adopting the position over the poles. The stirrups should be shortened by a couple of holes to help the rider feel secure when he is out of the saddle. No attempt should be made to jump anything until the rider has found his balance.

Once the rider has mastered trotting over poles he can progress to jumping cavalletti which are poles fixed either end to stands in the shape of a cross. The photographs on the two following pages show a grey pony jumping over cavalletti. These serve many purposes, as they can be used singly at varying heights or built up to form several types of jump of different heights and spreads. Practising over cavalletti will develop the correct jumping position. The rider will learn to find his balance and strength, feel the rhythm of the horse and be able to judge the horse's stride.

The cavalletti can be placed similarly to the poles in the diagram above, at their lowest size. When the rider has become confident at trotting over them while keeping firm control of the horse, he can gradually heighten and widen the poles, making sure that as he jumps he allows his body to move forward, then come back again as the horse lands.

It is essential that the rider feels completely in control at all times. He must practise turning before and after the fence and pulling up to a halt so that control is never lost

The variety of jumps in cross country riding gives the experienced rider plenty of opportunity to practise his skills. The rider is wearing a special safety hat used for racing and cross country riding, and is demonstrating a good position for jumping, his weight out of the saddle and well forward over the horse's neck, and his hands maintaining a firm control on short reins   ▶

The rider's position over fences

On take-off the rider's hands start to move forward, following the horse's head and maintaining a light contact on the reins

The rider has become left behind. Instead of allowing his hands to go forward, he has pulled the reins and caught the horse in the mouth

▲ As the horse approaches the take-off spot, he lowers his head and stretches his neck. As his fore legs lift up, he brings his hind legs underneath him. The rider is leaning forward taking the weight out of the saddle and on to his knee and thigh down into his heel. He has allowed his arms and hands to go forward, giving with the reins and following the horse's head

▲ The horse's hind legs have thrust him upwards and forward into the air. The rider has made sure before he attempted the jump that his stirrups were sufficiently short for him to maintain the same position and his balance throughout. He is following the movement and rhythm of the horse and allowing his arms and hands to go forward as the horse needs more rein

The position of the rider as the horse takes off, goes over the fence and lands is essential to the success of the jump. A wrong position at the beginning will affect the rest of the jump. If the position is wrong over the fence, it will affect the way the horse lands.

When trotting or cantering towards the fence, sit as still as possible, your body leaning slightly forward, the weight being taken on the knee and thigh down into the heel. The stirrups should be slightly shortened so that you can maintain this position easily and keep your balance while moving with the rhythm of the horse. You must not straighten your knee when attempting to stand up in the stirrup irons.

As the horse approaches the take-off spot, his head will lower slightly as his hind legs move underneath him before thrusting off upwards and over the fence. Your hands and arms should follow the horse's head, maintaining a light contact on the reins throughout but at no time

▲ This little grey pony and young rider jump confidently over cavalletti in nice style. The rider is leaning well forward, so that his weight is taken out of the saddle and on to his legs, and his arms and hands are giving with the reins, allowing the horse unrestricted movement of his head

While the horse is at full stretch in the air, the rider allows his hands and arms to go further forward to give more rein

As the horse lands, the rider braces his weight through his legs and brings his hands back to the normal position

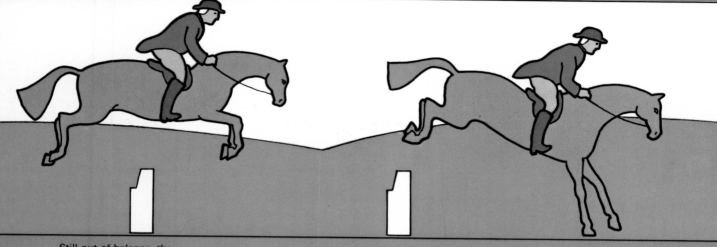

Still out of balance, the rider is restricting the freedom of the horse's head, forcing him to jump flat and possibly knock the fence

On landing, the rider has allowed his body to be thrust right back and his legs to shoot forward, completely out of balance

▲ The horse's head and neck are stretched out to the full extent, slightly downwards, and his hind legs are being gathered up underneath him as he clears the fence. The rider maintains his balance and ensures the horse is being given unrestricted movement of his head by keeping a light contact on the reins as he prepares to land

▲ As the horse lands, his head comes up and his neck shortens as he balances himself. The rider braces his weight through his legs and allows them to come very slightly forward to take the landing. He is bringing his hands back to the normal position as the horse completes a perfect jump

▲ Although this rider has allowed himself to become a little left behind the movement of his horse – his body is not well enough forward, so his weight is still in the saddle – he has at least given sufficient rein for the horse to complete the jump unrestricted

restricting the horse's movement.

On landing, the horse's head will come up and his neck shorten as he balances himself, and your hands and arms should move back into the normal position.

It is essential that your legs remain on the girths throughout. If you allow them to slip forwards or backwards, you will unbalance the whole movement and find it difficult to maintain your weight through the stirrups.

Practise the jumping position over small fences at both the trot and canter and, once mastered, progress to jumping two fences in a row. In between the two fences return to the pre-jumping position to balance the horse and do not allow yourself to slip or remain too far forward after each fence.

Jump for joy
On to larger fences

Once you can happily jump cavalletti, with practice you will be able to clear larger fences and the various types.

Never jump for too long, however, even though you need plenty of practice. The horse can become bored doing the same thing too often, so vary your jumps, not just by making the fences bigger but by attempting wider ones, such as parallel bars or a row of straw bales or oil drums on their sides. Whatever type of fence you attempt, make sure it is safe and has no nails sticking out. Be careful not to leave the cups (hooks) on uprights if there is not a pole up, as these can easily catch you or the horse.

When jumping larger fences try to gauge your take-off spot as you approach by looking at the ground line of the fence. A solid fence is easier to jump than rails and parallels because both horse and rider can see the ground line and judge the take-off spot from it. A rough guide to the correct take-off spot for an average-sized fence is its height as length along the ground.

Great accuracy is required to jump upright fences. When attempting parallels or wider fences it is important that the horse does not take off too far away or stand back.

Be careful not to attempt something too difficult for yourself or your horse. If things have gone wrong over a fence, either reduce its size, gradually building it up as you and the horse regain confidence, or jump a smaller fence before attempting the large one again.

The horse is jumping the fence fairly confidently and ▶ although the rider is a little too far back, she has managed to get her arms and hands forward enough to give with the reins and follow the horse's head

▲ As the horse approaches the fence at the beginning of the lesson the rider is still in the saddle. She is pushing down to urge the horse on and is giving enough rein for an unrestricted take-off

▲ The take-off was a little early but the rider has done well to bring herself forward in time for it. She is now going nicely with the horse, her weight off the saddle and her hands well forward on either side of the horse's neck

▲ The horse is being a little restricted as he lands because the rider has allowed herself to come back into the saddle, so putting weight on his quarters but she has avoided pulling his head with the reins

▲ The rider is now regaining her correct position and is sitting nicely balanced as the horse prepares to take the next stride

The different fences

There are numerous different types of fence ranging from uprights and parallels, walls and banks to ditches, hedges, gates and planks.

In show jumping great accuracy is required at all times to jump the fences clear and the horses must be trained to be obedient to the rider's every aid. Steeplechasers must be trained to jump at great speed safely and with the least possible effort. For cross country events the horses must be extremely bold and be trained to cope with every type of obstacle, such as the coffin which consists of two sets of posts and rails with a ditch in between, the Normandy bank which is a bank with a post and rails, and the bounce fence which is made up of sets of posts and rails positioned so closely together that there is no room for a full stride in between them.

The horses for America's Maryland Hunt Cup have to jump vast, solid fences of timber; those in Britain's daunting Grand National must be versatile enough to cope with Becher's Brook and the Chair.

A great deal can be achieved by jumping different fences when out riding. In order to become a good all-rounder, the horse must be adept at coping with every type of fence. He should learn how to jump up banks, over ditches and logs as well as over the more traditional show jumping fences.

▲ Both horse and rider appear confident as they make a big leap over a log, despite the fact that the take-off distance from it is a little long. Jumping natural fences, such as logs, ditches and hedges, is part of the requirement for competitive cross country riding

▼ This rider has stayed nicely with her horse as they jump out of the river. She is leaning forward over the horse's neck which is essential when jumping uphill. Horses tend to have a natural fear of water, so it is vital to accustom them to it, both for competitive and general riding purposes

▲ Jumping up banks needs tremendous impulsion and the rider must ensure she never gets left behind, or she will pull the horse back and off course. When coming down the bank, it is essential that the rider keeps the horse straight at all times, to ensure that he does not become unbalanced

▲ Water jumps in show jumping competitions particularly require great accuracy and impulsion. The horse must not be forced to stand back at this type of jump. He needs to take off close to it in order to clear the tape and not drop short into the water

▲ Clearing parallels needs practice and concentration, as the horse has to clear the width as well as the height. The rider must not make the mistake of looking at the back pole when approaching this type of jump or she may make her take-off too late and knock the first pole

▲ The wall is a favourite show jump and requires great accuracy. In Puissance Competitions the wall is raised to great heights and horses have cleared well over 2·13m (7ft). As with all uprights, the horse needs to get fairly close to the fence, in order to be able to spring vertically upwards

▲ Planks are considered to be the bogy fences. They are often hit, most probably because the horse's eye is distracted from the top of the fence by the colourful designs and also because they do not look imposing, as do solid fences which are respected much more by the horse

▲ Because gates are so upright, they are frequently knocked. They are also designed in such a way that even a fairly gentle touch will cause them to fall. Therefore a combination of great accuracy, impulsion and control is required if they are to be jumped clear

Riding for variety

Once you have mastered the basic arts of staying on, steering and control, a whole new world opens up to you. Riding is one of the few sports in which age makes little difference, as shown by the legendary Australian rider Bill Roycroft, who at sixty-two rode in the arduous Olympic Three-Day Event in 1976, and Britain's Lorna Johnstone, who at seventy rode in the Olympic Dressage Event in 1972.

You may wish just to enjoy hacking at weekends, a marvellous way to relax. If you are the competitive type, you may like to take part in events, such as gymkhanas for athletic children, show jumping, long-distance riding, hunter trials and one-day events. There is racing or point-to-pointing for those who enjoy riding at speed. Others may prefer to go pony trekking, or follow hounds out hunting. The dedicated rider may wish to learn dressage and achieve the ultimate in horse and rider training.

Whatever you decide to do, you will invariably be able to obtain the relevant information to start you on your way from an official horse society, details of which are given on page 123.

◀ Show jumping

Show jumping is one of the most popular of all equestrian sports. It requires great accuracy and skill from the rider and jumping ability from the horse. There are classes for all grades, starting with minimus jumping events for small children, where the height does not exceed 45·7cm (18in), and progressing through various grades and speed classes to the Puissance Class in which heights of over 2·13m (7ft) have been cleared. To do well, horses must be trained to jump all types of single and combination fence and be used to fences of any colour, shape and size.

Bareback riding ▶

This is great fun, especially on a nice, fat pony which is far more comfortable than the skinny type with a prominent backbone! For gymkhana events the rider must be able to ride bareback, keeping his balance and steering and controlling the pony when galloping. He is also required to vault on and off both when the pony is standing and when he is moving. The mane becomes a useful brace in helping to maintain balance. Before attempting to ride bareback, the rider should make sure the pony is quiet and there is someone to help if he gets into difficulties.

◀ Gymkhana

In a gymkhana children have a real chance to let off steam, as musical sacks, bending and relay races are won and lost in an atmosphere of intense excitement. Nearly all events are competed for bareback, and hard work and practice for all the events are sure to bring their rewards. In Britain the ambition of all young riders is to qualify to compete for the Prince Philip Cup which is held yearly at Wembley. Most teams are formed from those in the Pony Club, details of which are given on page 123.

Dressage ▶

This is the ultimate in the training of horse and rider on the flat. It is divided into several grades for both children and adults. In its most novice form horse and rider are expected to perform a series of set movements in an arena, for which marks are awarded by the judge. As the horse progresses, he may be entered for more advanced tests, the highest being the Grand Prix which is included in all championships and the Olympic Games. Dressage is also the first of the three phases in eventing, and Combined Training Events consist of dressage and show jumping.

Competition code

If you are entering a competition through your riding school, all arrangements will usually be made for you, including entry fees, transport, equipment and food.

If you are competing with your own horse, you will need to refer to the following subjects in the book: bandaging and loading into a trailer, pages 76-79; feeding, pages 92-93; grooming, rugs and blankets, and care of tack, pages 100-105; and first aid, pages 114-115.

When competing in any event, your horse must be clean, neat and tidy. Give him a thorough grooming and wash his mane and tail, and take your grooming kit for a final brush-over.

Your tack must be spotless, with all metalwork polished. Take a sponge, saddle soap and cloth with you for last-minute cleaning.

Your clothes must also be clean, neat and tidy and packed where they will not get covered with hay or damaged during the journey.

Make sure you take enough rugs with you if the weather is cold, and adequate food and

The preparation

water for the day. A well filled haynet and a small feed are all that are usually necessary at a one-day show. A full water-container is vital, as water is often either difficult to obtain or totally unavailable. If the weather is hot, give your horse extra water but do not offer it too soon before the competition. Likewise, do not let your horse eat too much just before competing in an energetic event.

It is advisable to bandage your horse's legs and tail for protection against injury while travelling. For small injuries that may occur during the day, take a simple first aid kit with you, which should include disinfectant, cotton wool, antibiotic wound powder or spray, gamgee and a bandage.

Allow yourself plenty of time for your journey to the competition and for getting yourself organized once you are there. You will need time to change, make final preparations to your horse's appearance, go to the secretary for your number and look at the layout.

▼ The ponies have been unloaded from their trailers and horseboxes at the competition ground and the riders now attend to last-minute preparations

This horse is well prepared for travelling, his legs ▶ bandaged and his knees protected by knee caps. The sheet, to keep him warm, is secured with a roller

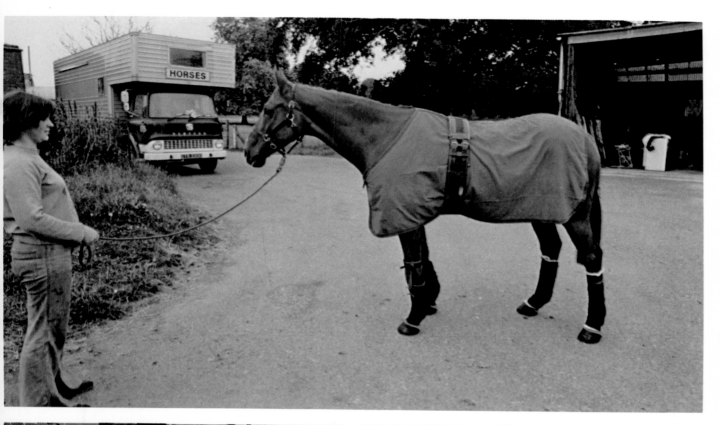

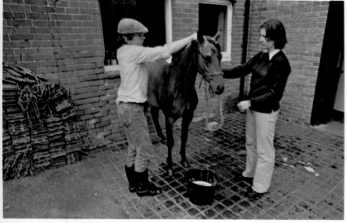

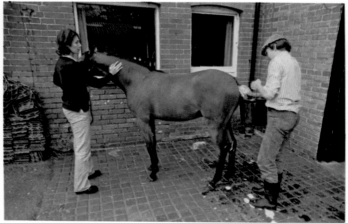

Washing a mane

First gather together all the equipment you will need: two buckets of warm water, two sponges, mild shampoo, a sweat scraper (see page 100) and towel. If the horse is quiet, tie him up; if he is a little excitable, have an assistant hold him in a head collar or halter.

Wet the mane thoroughly, then put a little shampoo on the sponge and rub it well into the mane and over the forelock, being careful not to let soap or water into the ears or eyes. Rinse the mane with the clean sponge and water. Remove excess water from the neck with the sweat scraper and rub the mane well with the towel.

Washing a tail

You will need the same equipment as for the mane. If the horse is quiet he can be tied up; otherwise he should be held by an assistant.

Talk quietly to the horse while you lift up the bucket of warm water and put the tail inside. Wash it thoroughly with the shampoo and sponge, rubbing the dock as well as the end of the tail so that it is clean from top to bottom. Rinse thoroughly with the clean sponge and water, then swish the tail round and round to remove excess water, and rub with the towel.

Competition code
Lunging

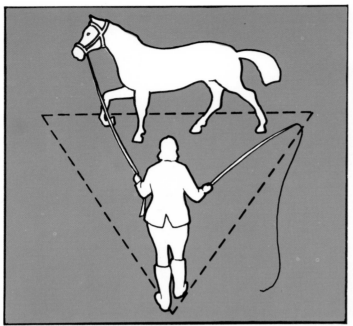

▲ The trainer is in the correct position for lunging a horse, creating the shape of a triangle. With the lunge rein held in her left hand and the lunge whip in her right, she is keeping the horse on a large circle and guiding him forward by swishing the whip towards his quarters

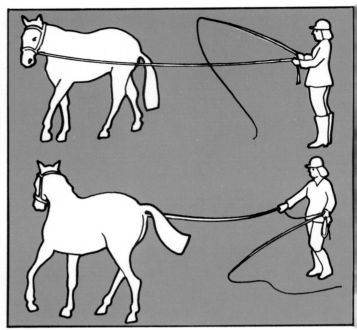

▲ The horse should be lunged on both reins for the same length of time, so that he remains supple on both sides. The horse is wearing a strong head collar and the diagram demonstrates clearly how to lunge the horse on the rein while guiding him forward by means of the lunge whip

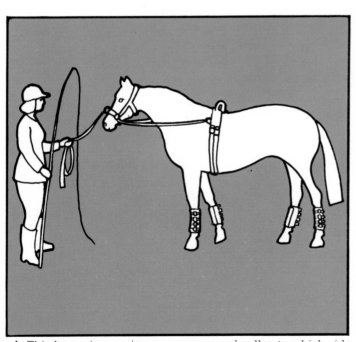

▲ This horse is wearing a cavesson and roller to which side reins are attached to keep the horse's head straight. They should be adjusted so that they are not too tight but the inner rein should be a couple of holes shorter than the outer, to allow the horse to bend naturally in the direction he is going on the circle. He is also wearing boots to protect his legs from knocks and bruises. The horse's legs, especially the fore legs, should always be protected when lunging either by boots or exercise bandages

When a horse is trained in the conventional way, lunging on a long rein on a circle is usually the first lesson he learns before being ridden. The object of lunging is to teach the horse three main things: to answer the trainer's voice, obedience and free forward movement.

The voice is one of the aids of riding and once the horse understands a vocal instruction from the rider, he will respond to it more readily than to the often confusing signals from the beginner's hands and legs. Obedience means self-control by the horse, a curbing of his natural exuberance so that he learns instead to carry out the wishes of his trainer. Free forward movement is shown by suppleness in the back, a swinging tail and flowing paces performed without hesitation.

Later on, lunging can be used for further training of the horse or corrective training if he has been spoilt by bad riding. By relearning on the lunge, much of the damage caused can be corrected in knowledgeable hands.

Lunging can also be used for exercise if, for some reason such as a sore back, the horse should not be ridden. When the excitement of a competition has temporarily rendered the horse unsuitable for its rider, twenty minutes or so on the lunge will normally be all that is necessary to return the animal to its usual accommodating self.

It is with these last two reasons for lunging that

▲ This bay yearling colt is wearing protective exercise bandages on his fore legs. The trainer is standing quite still, forming the shape of a triangle with the horse, and keeping him out on a circle on the lunge rein, while guiding him forward with the lunge whip

the beginner should concern himself, so that he will know enough to be able to help both himself and his horse.

The basic equipment needed to lunge a horse is as follows: a lunging head collar or cavesson, the name given to an extra strong head collar, so designed that it cannot pull into the horse's eyes; a lunge rein which is a long rein usually made of webbing or canvas and is fastened to the rings on the nose band of the cavesson or to the underside of a head collar; a lunge whip which is used not to hit the horse but with a swishing action to guide the horse forward. A roller to which side reins are attached and joined to the cavesson can also be used. The side reins help to keep the horse's head straight when being lunged but care must be taken to ensure that the inner rein is slightly shorter than the outer, so that the horse can bend naturally in the direction he is going on the circle. Strong binder twine or an old pair of reins make adequate side reins.

Exercise bandages (see page 76) or boots, as shown in the diagram opposite, should always be worn by the horse when lunging, for protection against knocks and bruises. Protective boots are made of leather, felt or plastic and have buckles which should be fastened on the outside; the ends of the straps should point backwards so that they do not rub or catch on the horse's legs.

To lunge your horse take him to a quiet corner of a field or find some enclosed area where there are not too many distractions. Hold the lunge rein looped in your left hand, together with the lunge whip. Release the rein gradually, letting the horse move away from you in a large circle, then transfer the whip to your right hand and point it towards his quarters to encourage him to move forward and remain out on the circle. Keep guiding the horse forward by swishing the whip towards him; it should seldom be necessary to hit him with it.

If you have an inexperienced horse on the lunge, it is useful to have an assistant who can lead him out on the circle while you remain in the centre to guide him forward with the whip.

Use the voice to ask the horse to walk, trot, canter and halt, making sure you use the same words of command each time. Execute all movements quietly, never jerking the reins but maintaining an even contact throughout, and do not allow a loop to form on which the horse could tread. Remember it is the horse that should be moving and not you, so remain in the same spot all the time, forming the point of a triangle.

The horse must be lunged in both directions, so that he remains supple on both sides. Never lunge a horse for too long; half an hour is sufficient for most horses doing normal work.

To make the horse slow down, lower the whip and if necessary give a few pulls on the rein until the pace decreases, and at the end of the session again lower the whip first before looping the rein.

Competition code
Plaiting

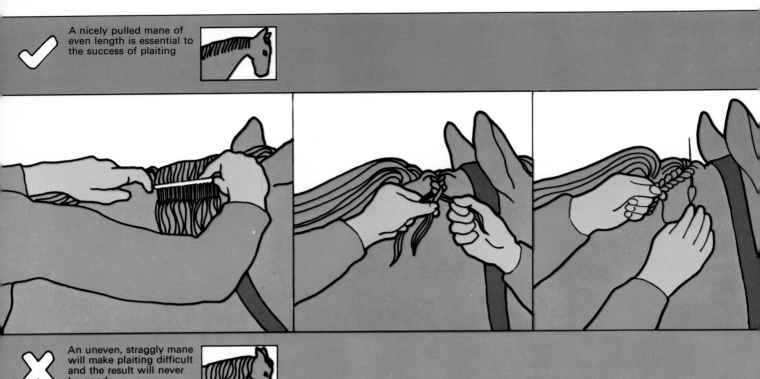

A nicely pulled mane of even length is essential to the success of plaiting

An uneven, straggly mane will make plaiting difficult and the result will never be good

▲ Having ensured that the mane is nicely pulled and of an even length, start at the top and damp it using the water brush, then measure the size of plait you want with the mane comb. Plaits look neater if they are small, so do not take too large a piece of mane

▲ Divide your measured piece into three sections and start plaiting, keeping a firm hold until you are about 2·5cm (1in) from the end. Turn the end under, wind thread round to bind the bottom, then push the needle through the binding to secure the thread

▲ Fold the plait under once, then push the needle through the top of the mane, taking care not to stab the horse. Pull the thread tight and you now have a loop. Pass the needle back and through the mane again to secure the loop

Plaiting is done to improve the horse's appearance for such occasions as a show, a competition or a day's hunting. It can be done in several ways – in some countries it is called braiding – but whichever way you choose, you will achieve success only if you ensure before you start that the mane is nicely pulled and of an even length. How to pull and tidy a mane is described on page 97.

Plaiting can be finished off with thread or elastic bands. Thread should always be used in preference, as it keeps the plaits tighter, so giving them a more professional look but for minor events elastic bands are adequate.

The tail can also be plaited but for this to be a success, the horse needs a full tail to start with and you need a great deal of practice before showing off your handiwork in public.

Before you start to plait, gather all the necessary equipment together and tie up your horse securely where there is plenty of good light. You will need a blunt needle, such as a darning needle, with thread attached and knotted at the end, a mane comb and water brush (see page 100) and a bucket of water. If the horse is big, you may need a feed bin or bale of straw on which to stand. Make sure you have extra thread and a pair of scissors. Always attach the needle and scissors to something where they can be easily seen. If they dropped or became lost, they could cause a lot of damage.

Plait the mane following the diagrams and instructions above. Make sure the plaits are secured neatly and firmly and that the distance between each one is the same throughout. Plaiting can be done by an experienced person in twenty minutes to half an hour but the beginner should allow much more time.

The mane of the chestnut show pony has been beautifully ▶ worked into small, evenly sized, well spaced plaits and the youthful appearance of the bay yearling colt has been considerably tidied up by his plaited tail

74

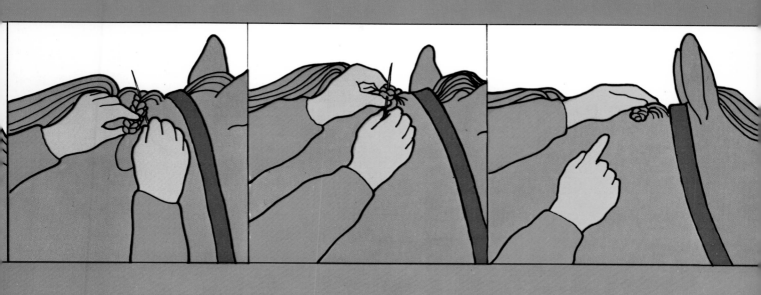

▲ Fold the loop up and push the needle again through the top of the mane. Pull the thread tight. A neat button may now have formed but if not it will be necessary to make a third loop by following the same procedure as for the second

▲ Once you have a neat button, push the needle and thread up and down the plait to keep it firm, then cut the thread making sure you do not cut any of the mane. Never cut off any mane that is left sticking out after you have completed the plait

▲ The first plait is complete and you can now move on to the next. The size of the horse and the reason for the plaiting governs the number you need but 10-12 is a good average. Whatever the occasion, plaits should be neat, regularly spaced and of the same size

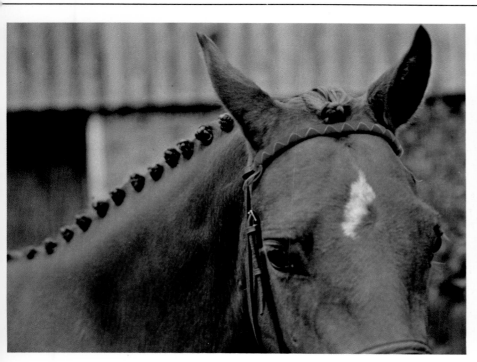

Bandaging

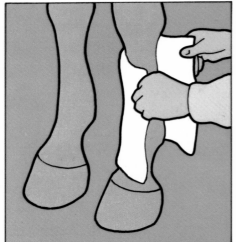

▲ Before applying the stable bandage, used for protection and warmth, cut a piece of gamgee long enough to fit from below the knee to the foot and wide enough to go once round the leg

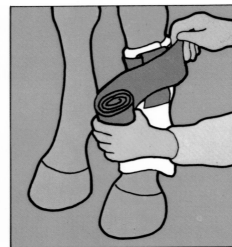

▲ Place the end of the bandage, angled upwards, just below the knee. Take the bandage round one turn, then let the end fall over it. Take the bandage round again and over the end

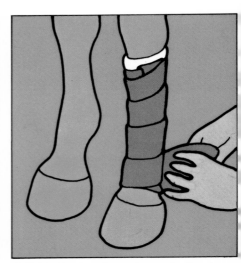

▲ Take the bandage down the leg in even turns, over the fetlock joint and round the pastern. When the coronet is reached, you can start taking the bandage back up the leg

▲ For exercise bandages, cut a piece of gamgee to fit from below the knee to the fetlock. Wrap it round the leg, then start bandaging following the procedure for the stable bandage

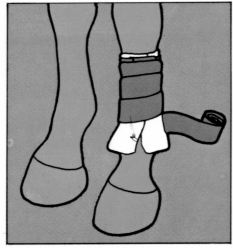

▲ Take the bandage down the leg until it just reaches the fetlock joint. It is essential that this type of bandage is applied firmly and evenly to support the leg but not hinder the circulation

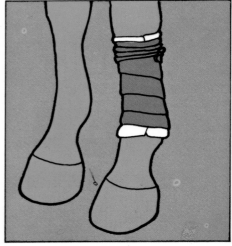

▲ The bandage is taken back up the leg to the starting place and the tapes tied in the same way as for the stable bandage. For competition work the knot should be sewn to the bandage

Stable bandages, usually made of wool, are used for protection against injury, for instance when travelling, or for warmth and comfort after a long, hard day. They should cover as much of the leg as possible, from the hock or knee downwards and should have a layer of gamgee (cotton wool enclosed in lint) underneath. The bandages should be put on firmly enough to ensure they stay in place but loosely enough not to hinder the circulation. Great care should be taken not to tie the tapes too tightly, as they could injure the horse's legs.

Exercise bandages, usually made of crepe or a similar elasticated material, are used for protection and support when lunging or when riding if the horse is inclined to knock himself or has bad action. They should be put on firmly and evenly from just below the knee to the fetlock and the tapes tied securely but not tightly. If you are unsure of your ability to apply this type of bandage correctly, you may feel it is safer to fit your horse with protective boots, as shown and described on pages 72-73.

Tail bandages, usually made of crepe, are

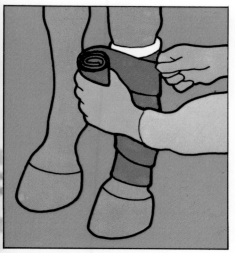

▲ Continue taking the bandage up the leg in even turns until you reach the starting place. Make sure you are not binding the bandage so tightly that the circulation is hindered

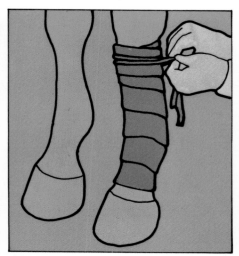

▲ Tie the tapes, ensuring they are not too tight and that the knot is on the inside or outside of the leg and not on the front or back where it will press on the bone or tendons

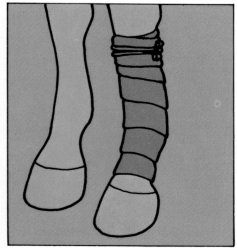

▲ Tuck in the spare ends of the tapes and the bandage is now complete, looking neat and tidy, and firm enough to stay in place and protect the leg against injury

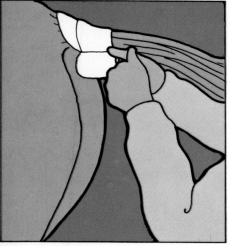

▲ Tail bandages are used for protection and to improve the appearance of the tail. Lift the dock of the tail and pass the bandage round in a couple of firm turns

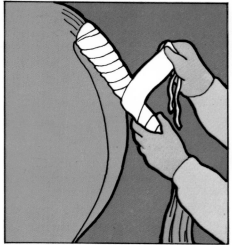

▲ Take the bandage down the tail in firm, even turns until it reaches the end of the dock. Then bring the bandage up again so that the tapes can be tied at about the midway point

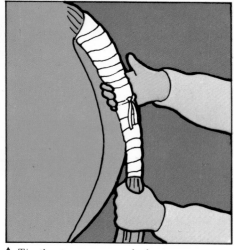

▲ Tie the tapes securely but not so tightly that the circulation is hindered, at the point illustrated in the diagram or just below the dock. Gently pull the tail into a natural shape

used for protection, especially when travelling, and to improve the appearance of the tail. The tapes should be tied firmly but not too tightly either below the dock or half way up the tail. Tail guards made of wool or leather can also be used. These go over the tail bandage, giving extra protection, and are fastened to a roller to keep them in place.

This horse's legs are protected with stable bandages neatly and firmly applied. The knot is on the outside of the leg and the tapes have been tucked in. The gamgee beneath the bandage is clearly visible at top and bottom ▶

Loading into a trailer

◄ The partition has been removed from this trailer as only one horse is travelling. The floor has been covered with straw to prevent him from slipping and a little strewn on the ramp to make it look more inviting. The haynet is already in place, tied securely to a tie-ring

▲ The horse is being led quietly into the trailer and an assistant will close the ramp once the horse is safely in. The horse is well protected against possible injury with stable bandages and gamgee and a tail bandage, and he is being kept warm with a sheet secured by a roller

Loading a horse is seldom a problem. Most well travelled horses can be led quite happily into a trailer or horsebox, so long as they have not been frightened in the past when travelling or have not had an unfortunate experience immediately before being loaded. The problems of loading are discussed on pages 56-57.

First ensure that the floor of the trailer is prepared with straw or shavings to prevent the horse from slipping about, and place a little on the ramp to make it look more inviting. Check that the trailer is properly hitched to the car, with the safety catch secured to stop it tipping up as the horse goes in. If your horse is to travel with a haynet, attach it to a tie-ring in the front of the trailer. Make sure it is tied securely and fairly high up, so that there is no risk of the horse getting his foot caught in it.

Horses should be protected from injury when travelling by bandages with gamgee and a tail bandage. Small, naturally well protected ponies may not need this protection. If it is cold, a rug should be put on (see pages 102-103).

Lead the horse by his head collar or halter, giving yourself plenty of room to walk straight in. Walk up the ramp and tie him to a piece of string which should be attached to a tie-ring. This is safer than tying him directly to the ring, for if he panics he will then only break the string and not injure himself too severely. Secure him with a safety knot on a fairly short rope so that he cannot swing about too much when the vehicle moves. Talk to him while you are doing this and give him a few nuts if he needs encouragement.

Unless you know that your horse is a good loader, it is always wise to have a helper to close the ramp as soon as the horse is in. You can then come out through the groom's side-door after you have checked that the horse is secure.

Many trailers have webbing straps at the back which can be fastened across as soon as the horse has loaded. These should always be used, as they prevent the horse from rushing out backwards, which can become a bad habit, or he

▲ While the assistant closes up the ramp, the leader makes sure that the horse is comfortable and gives him a few nuts if he needs some encouragement. Having checked that the horse is attached securely to the tie-ring, she can come out through the groom's side-door

may get frightened for some reason and his natural instinct will be to back out.

Horses should always be secured when travelling. Leaving them loose is dangerous, as they could try to jump out. However, small ponies which cannot see out may be left loose if they travel better that way.

To take the horse out of the trailer, it may be possible to turn him round and lead him, depending on his size. If not, first untie him so that he is loose and will not injure himself should he rush backwards. Get someone to open the ramp then, holding on to his rope, slowly and quietly push into his chest to make him reverse down the ramp. If he rushes back, let him have as much rope as possible, otherwise he may throw his head up and hit it on the trailer roof.

When towing trailers, the driver must brake and accelerate as smoothly as possible, avoiding any jerky movements and being particularly careful when cornering, so that he does not swing the horse about and frighten him.

Oiling the feet

Although oiling the feet is part of the general necessary day-to-day care, it is essential that it is done just before the horse is due to travel. Not only does it improve the appearance but it also helps to protect the foot. A horse's feet take a lot of punishment, having to cope with hard and soft ground, rough and smooth.

The feet should be washed if necessary. The hoof oil is then applied with a brush (see page 100) first to the frog and sole and then to the outside, right up to the coronet.

Mountain and Moorland Ponies

The British Mountain and Moorland Ponies are unique. There are nine breeds from different parts of the British Isles, ranging from the smallest, the Shetland from the Shetland Isles, to the largest and strongest, the Highland from Scotland. In between are the Connemara which although from Eire is generally considered to be a British breed; the Fell and Dales from the north of England; the New Forest, Exmoor and Dartmoor from the south and west; and probably the most popular of all, the various types of Welsh pony.

They are in great demand all over the world, as they are renowned for their toughness, intelligence and suitability as children's riding ponies. They are all extremely hardy, living out in cold weather all the year round as did their predecessors back to prehistoric times. Their cause and welfare is governed by the National Pony Society (see page 123), the oldest society of its kind in the world.

By cross-breeding some Mountain and Moorland Ponies with the Thoroughbred, some fine riding ponies and horses have been produced and have been extremely successful, not only in the show ring but also in the eventing and show jumping circles.

▲ The Welsh Ponies and Cobs are divided into different height sections. This pony, showing the typical classic head of the breed, is a Section B which does not exceed 1·37m (13·2 hands)

The Fell is similar to the Dales Pony ▶ pictured overleaf but it is finer in type and there is more variance in height. In the past they carried lead from the mines in northern England

◀ Shetland Ponies are probably the oldest and certainly the smallest of Britain's native breeds, being on average no more than 1·01m (40in). Well handled they make ideal first ponies for children

The Highland, strongest and ▶ sturdiest of the British breeds, is known for its excellent temperament. They are still used to bring game down from the hills

▼ The sturdy, agile Exmoor, believed to be a descendant of the British Wild Horse, is distinguishable from all other breeds by its 'mealy' eyes, caused by a rim encircling them

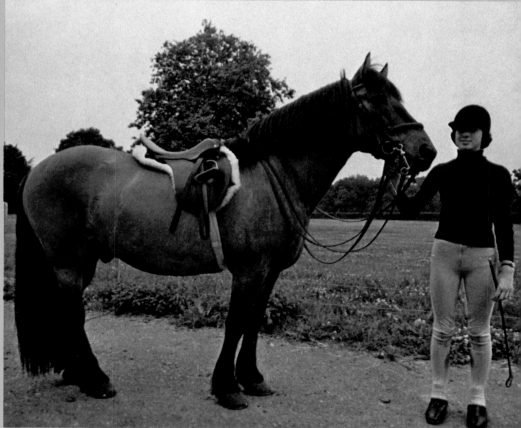

▲ The Dartmoor Pony, first mentioned in the year 1012, was used between the tenth and twelfth centuries to carry tin from the moor. Measuring under 1·27m (12·2 hands), they look like miniature hunters and are much sought after all over the world as children's ponies

The New Forest Pony is one of the largest of the British ▶ breeds. Because of their temperaments, these ponies are probably the most suitable of all for children. They are hardy, good in traffic, extremely sure-footed and less shy of people than any other breed

▼ The Welsh Mountain Pony is renowned for its intelligence, kind temperament, courage and outstandingly pretty head which is slightly dish-faced, similar to that of the Arab. This is a Section A Pony, the smallest of all the sections, not exceeding 1·21m (12 hands)

▼ The Welsh Cob, as his name suggests, is larger, hardier and stronger than the Welsh Ponies, measuring over 1·37m (13·2 hands). He is sure-footed, alert and active, making an ideal type for a family pony. Although he is a little strong, with training he can become quite safe for children

▼ The Dales Pony, usually black in colour, is extremely strong for his size and at one time was used in the mines. They are hard-working ponies, active yet docile. They make excellent harness ponies as well as riding ponies and are ideal for children

▼ Legend has it – though it is much disputed – that the Connemara Ponies from the Galway region of Eire crossed with some of the horses that swam ashore from the wrecked Spanish Armada in 1588. They have lovely temperaments, so are extremely popular as children's riding ponies

A horse of your own

Buying a horse

Once you have taken up riding and have found that you enjoy the sport, you may decide that you would like to own a horse or pony. However, there are many things to consider before you come to your decision.

There are the practical aspects to consider first. Do you have the facilities for a horse or pony? You will need land or stables. Do you have enough time to devote to his care? He needs to be looked after or checked daily, whether grass- or stable-kept. Have you had any experience in looking after a horse or pony? You will need to obtain as much information as possible, either from reading all you can or taking advice from those who have experience.

Owning a horse or pony is not only a big responsibility, it is also expensive. The cost of buying him is just the start. In addition to land or stabling, he will need shelter if he is to be kept out and sufficient bedding if stabled. You will need clothing in which to ride him; he will need tack in which to be ridden. You will need equipment to look after him, and food and water with which to feed him. He will need shoeing and occasional care from the vet.

If your horse or pony is to be kept out at grass, you must ensure that the fencing is safe and adequate and this must be inspected regularly. There must be a continuous supply of fresh water available and some form of shelter. A tree may be all that is necessary for him to stand under out of the heat of the sun or in the cold of winter, but ideally a shed should be supplied, preferably fitted out with a manger for food. If the grass is past its best, for instance at the end of the summer, a plentiful supply of good, old hay will be necessary, and some form of feed if the horse or pony is in work or the weather is bad. A small pony will probably need only hay.

If you are contemplating keeping your horse or pony in a stable, he will require feeding at regular times, plenty of fresh water, a good grooming each day and a clean, dry bed at night. The stable will need to be kept scrupulously clean and mucked out daily. The advantage of keeping a pony stabled is that he is always to hand when you want to ride him. A grass-kept pony first has to be caught.

Once you have carefully considered all these points, have decided you would be happy to take on the responsibility of ownership and are sure you have all the facilities essential to a pony's care, you will need to consider the type of horse or pony suitable for your needs.

He should be the right size for you and this is best judged by your mounting him. You will soon be able to feel and see whether he is too big or small. It is as well to remember that a horse under five years old is unsuitable for the beginner. If he is a first pony, you will not need him to be too highly bred. Whether you are going to keep him in a stable or at grass also has some bearing on the type. A hardy pony can be kept at grass all year round. A horse will need to be stabled during the colder months. Lastly and vitally important, you must ensure that he has a good temperament and is free from vice.

There are several ways to choose from when tackling the task of finding a suitable horse or pony but in almost every case, seek the advice of a knowledgeable friend. If possible, ask him to accompany you when you go to see a horse you intend to buy, to give you his opinion. Failing that, your local branch of the Pony or Riding Club (see page 123) will always give help and guidance. Before you make your final decision, have the horse vetted for soundness by your vet. The ways of buying open to you are as follows: you can go to a horse sale, answer advertisements, buy through a reputable horse dealer or buy a pony already known to you.

Horse sales are usually advertised in the equestrian magazines. A list of the horses being offered is usually made available a few weeks before the given date. Make sure you obtain it and study the details before you go along.

Answering the advertisements in the equestrian press is often a successful way of buying a horse. Telephone or write to the seller to obtain all the necessary details before making your journey to see the horse. Watch the horse being ridden, then ride him yourself.

If you know exactly what sort of horse you require, you can go to a horse dealer, who makes his living by finding the right horse for his customer.

Buying a pony that is already known to you is obviously less of a problem than any other way of buying. You will know his temperament and ways and be familiar with his performance. The reason he is to be sold may be that the rider has outgrown him and so the seller will be just as concerned as you are about the purchase.

Once you have bought your horse, it is wise to obtain insurance. Several companies specialize in horse insurance (see page 123), so approach them for the necessary information.

Happiness is having a pony all of your own! ▶

Looking after your horse

▲ A bowl of food and head collar and rope are being taken to catch this piebald mare in her well fenced paddock, sheltered by a large tree. The owner is approaching quietly, walking towards the mare's shoulder. Many ponies will come to be caught when called by name

▲ When a halter is used, it is essential that a knot is tied in the rope, as shown in this diagram. This ensures that only the knot tightens if the horse pulls back. Without the knot, the halter would tighten round the horse's nose and cause possible injury to his jaw

Once you have bought your horse, you need to ensure that you have the special equipment necessary for his care.

A halter or head collar and rope with which to lead your horse is the first requirement. Then comes the question of tack. A saddle, girths, stirrup irons and leathers, bridle and neck strap make up the basic necessary tack which is covered in detail on pages 18-19. You also need some rugs and blankets, and a roller to secure them (see pages 102-103), grooming equipment (see page 100) and a tack-cleaning kit (see pages 104-105).

The stabled horse, which is discussed in detail on pages 90-91, needs a constant supply of bedding, a haynet unless there is already a hayrack in the stable, a feed bowl and a good-sized water bucket. Two may be necessary, as horses drink 27-45 litres (6-10 gallons) of water a day. All feed stuffs should be stored in a dry place and preferably in a vermin-proof container. To muck out the stable you need a fork, rake, shovel, broom and wheelbarrow or dung sack. These complete the list of essential.

▲ Ponies like to be kept together in a field or paddock. In groups they provide each other with company and shelter, and by standing head to tail they can give one another a good scratch, just as these two are doing, and swish away the flies with their tails

requirements for the stabled horse, which can be modified for the grass-kept pony.

When looking after a stabled horse a routine should be set and rigidly adhered to. Horses are creatures of habit and thrive better when they are fed, groomed and exercised at the same times every day.

A typical daily routine for the average horse doing Riding Club activities might be as follows:

7.15a.m.   Muck out stable and feed horse. Put tack ready for exercise. Tidy yard or stable area. Fill water buckets, straighten rugs.

9a.m.   Brush horse over. Take him out for exercise or turn him out to grass. On return, provide hay. Clean tack. Groom the horse if he is dry. Check water.

12.30p.m.   Pick up droppings. Water and feed. Provide more hay if necessary. Leave the horse to rest or turn him out to grass.

5p.m.   If the horse was not groomed before, do this now. Pick up droppings. Provide more hay and water. Feed and put rugs on for the night.

9p.m.   Check water and rugs. Provide more hay if necessary. Horses in strong work may have an extra feed.

This programme can, of course, be altered to suit your hours, depending on the amount of time you have to care for your horse. The important thing is to stick to the routine you have set and to ensure that if the horse is being fed two or more feeds, they are planned so that he is not left for too long a period of time without food. If the horse is having only two feeds, these should be given morning and evening. Feeding a stabled horse is discussed on pages 92-93.

The grass-kept pony, which is discussed in detail on the following page, needs little special attention, apart from a good supply of fresh water, a daily check-over and feed during the cold months, four- to six-weekly visits to the blacksmith, and worming approximately every six weeks (see page 96). Ponies should be turned out together if possible. This not only provides them with company but in groups they shelter one another and, by standing head to tail in hot weather, they are able to swish the flies from each other.

A horse of your own
At grass

With a little knowledge and some common sense you should have no problems in keeping a horse or pony at grass. Because ponies are hardy, they can be kept at grass all year round; horses should be stabled during the cold months. Both ponies and horses kept at grass should be checked daily.

Before you turn your pony out to grass, check that the field has good, safe fencing, that all the gates shut securely and are fitted with padlocks if they open out on to the road. Remove any sharp objects, which your pony could tread on, and poisonous plants, such as yew, ragwort and rhododendrons.

A good supply of fresh water should be available in the field. This can be a running stream, so long as it is sufficiently deep and easily accessible, or an automatically filled water trough which should be checked daily, cleaned out as necessary and the ice broken daily during the cold weather. Ponds are not a suitable source, as they hold stagnant water.

Shelter of some sort is essential. Even a slight hedge will act as a windbreak but a three-sided shed will be more welcome, and hay can be fed more satisfactorily under a roof than on open ground. Many animals will not shelter in a shed from rain or snow but will appreciate it much more during the summer as an escape from the sun and the flies.

If it is possible, turn two ponies out to grass together. Company is always appreciated but it is vital that the two are friends, so that a kicking match and veterinary bill are not the result. If there is any doubt, have the hind shoes removed first. Some people say ponies settle better if they are turned out in the evening but they usually get on well, so long as there is no extra food around for them to argue over. If you have to give them extra food, make sure it is placed well apart.

Grass is at its best during the spring when it can be quite rich, but this richness in protein can cause the condition called laminitis, particularly in small ponies, which is an inflammation of the sensitive laminae in the feet (see pages 112-113). Ponies prone to this condition should be brought in either during the day or at night, kept on short food rations and given bran mashes daily (see page 92).

In winter grass has little food-value. Although ponies may be happy and remain looking well, extra feeding is necessary as the cold weather sets in (see pages 92-93), and hay must always be given during frosty and snowy conditions.

If there is any slight deterioration in the pony's condition, extra food must be given to counteract this. Horses in this condition will also need extra feeding with hay and probably horse and pony nuts or a similar complete and well balanced food, as an additional measure.

If your pony is kept in a small paddock, the droppings should be picked up daily to prevent the land becoming horse-sick and to help ease the problem of worm infestation. If it is possible, arrange for a few cows to graze off the rough grass which the pony will not eat. This will do the ground good and sweeten the grass. Regular harrowing and a yearly lime dressing of some sort will also help to keep the land in good condition.

Care of the feet is just as important for ponies at grass as those kept stabled. Although the shoe gets little wear out in the field, the foot continues to grow. The shoe therefore gradually works forward on to the sole of the foot, causing a bruise called a corn, which can result in lameness (see page 112). Alternatively, the shoe may start to fall off and catch on the other feet, causing bruises or even a wound.

If your pony is not going to be ridden for some time, have the shoes removed and put on again when next you are going to ride. If the hooves become chipped or broken, get them rasped and trimmed by the blacksmith before serious cracks develop. Feet should always be attended to by the blacksmith every four to six weeks.

Worming is even more vital for the grass-kept pony than for the stabled horse. The eggs are being ingested daily with the grass. Flies lay their eggs on the pony and these will also be eventually ingested as the pony licks his coat. A worm dose is vital at least every six weeks if the health of your pony is to be maintained, and the type of dose should be varied three or four times a year (see page 96). Remember to have your pony's teeth checked yearly by the vet.

In freezing weather a New Zealand rug (see pages 102-103) should be put on a fine-skinned pony, so long as it is removed daily and a check made for any sore spots.

The grass-kept pony should never be groomed, as this removes the natural oils from his coat. Before riding a gentle brush-over and tidy-up are all that are needed.

Although this horse looks well, he is just starting to show ▶ signs of weight loss at the approach of autumn. The grass has already begun to lose its food-value, so extra feeding is now necessary

A horse of your own
The stabled horse

The stabled horse requires a fairly strict routine which should be varied as little as possible.

When you arrive in the morning, check that the horse has suffered no injury during the night, has eaten his feed and that there are the usual amount of droppings in his box. Straighten his rugs if necessary, then muck out the stable and feed and water him. Sawdust, shavings or peat moss are fairly easy to clean but straw takes a little more time. Make sure the bedding is as dry as possible and dig out any very damp patches, as wet bedding can harm the horse's feet. There should be plenty of bedding on the floor so that the horse will not injure himself when rolling or getting up and down during the night.

First thing in the morning is probably the best time to ride but this depends on when you have the time. Having exercised your horse or turned him out if he is not being ridden, groom him thoroughly (see pages 100-101) and refill his water bucket and haynet. Clean the tack (see pages 104-105), feed your horse if a midday feed is due and leave him to rest for the afternoon or turn him out to grass. At teatime tidy the stable, refill the water buckets and haynet and put on the night rugs. Give the largest feed at this time.

Later in the evening check the hay and water and pick up droppings. Give a final feed if the horse is in serious work, then check that all is well and that the tackroom is locked. Feeding is covered on the following two pages.

Once a week a bran mash (see page 92) with a tablespoon of Epsom salts should be given, to aid digestion. The horse should not be worked too hard on the day after this laxative feed.

When mucking out shavings, sawdust or peat moss, first pick up the droppings, then rake the box across, leaving the bed slightly higher at the sides. Add extra bedding when necessary.

When mucking out straw, start at the door and throw the clean straw to one side of the box. Slightly soiled straw will dry out and can be used again but very wet straw must be thrown out. When the whole bed has been sifted through, sweep the floor and if possible leave it for a time to dry before relaying the straw, adding clean straw when necessary and banking it well at the sides. Alternatively, muck out by using the deep litter system, which means that you add clean straw on top of the old when necessary, then dig the box out completely every six weeks or so.

Special attention must be paid to the feet of the stabled horse. They should be checked daily during the grooming session, picked out with a hoof pick (see pages 98-101) and inspected for

▼ Having been fed and watered, exercised and groomed, this horse is now being led out to grass for the afternoon

▲ A typical stable scene: horses are being led out for exercise through this clean, well organized stable, watched by a row of well-cared-for horses in their boxes, their heads well protected from the rain by the overhanging roof

any signs of thrush (see page 113) which can be caused by wet bedding.

Always check that your horse is warm enough during the winter months and be prepared to put on or take off an extra rug, depending on the severity of the weather. It is always better to add an extra rug rather than close a top door or window. Horses need plenty of fresh air but must not be subject to draughts.

Never leave a stabled horse in his box all day. He should always be given some form of exercise, even on his day off. A horse should have one easy day a week, preferably the day after his bran mash, during which he should simply be led to a field for a bit of grass.

One of the very few problems you may encounter with your stabled horse is a condition known as Azoturia, Set Fast or Monday Morning Disease. This is a seizing up of the muscles in the back and quarters and although the cause is not really known, it is associated with the stabled horse doing sudden work. How to cope with this problem is covered on page 115.

The horse is a creature of habit and to ensure that he or his system does not become upset, it is essential that any change in diet or exercise is done on a day-by-day, gradual programme.

The art of keeping your horse fit and healthy depends on three main things: good feeding, good exercise and good stable management.

To ensure good feeding your horse should be given the best quality food available, fed little and often and at regular times. Gradually increase the protein in accordance with an increase in work and avoid any sudden changes in diet.

Good exercise means a gradual progression in the amount of work, starting with slow, sedate exercise and gradually increasing it as the horse becomes fitter. Never overdo the amount of work before the horse is fit enough and never gallop or jump him before he is ready.

Good stable management and the ability to pay attention to detail will ensure that your stabled horse remains healthy and gives you many years of pleasure as you devote yourself to his welfare.

Feeding a stabled horse

Good feeding is an art acquired only after years of experience but modern methods make it easier for the beginner to do an adequate job. The basis of good feeding is little and often, as horses for their size have very small stomachs and in their natural state they eat only grass.

For best results, always buy the highest quality food available and feed according to the weight, age and amount of work your horse is doing. For instance, a horse being ridden every day will need more food than one being ridden only at weekends. In cold weather all horses need extra food to compensate for the energy lost in keeping themselves warm. Always water before feeding and feed at the same time each day.

Make sure that the type and amount of food you give suits your horse and alter it as and when necessary. For instance, if he is getting too fat, cut down on the amount of bulk feed. If he is too thin, increase the bulk feed. However, as with any change in diet, this should be done gradually, to allow the digestion to adjust.

Additional succulent foods, such as apples, turnips, freshly cut grass, dandelions and carrots (always cut lengthways so that they cannot become caught in the horse's gullet) are all favourites and will act as appetizers for shy feeders. Do not ride too soon after feeding. The horse needs at least an hour to digest his food.

Always make sure the manger or feed bin is clean. Stale food stuck to the edges will quickly put a horse off his feed. Any unfinished food should be removed before another feed is given.

For a well balanced diet a horse's feed must include protein, carbohydrate, fibre, salt and vitamins. These are all found in hay, bran, oats, barley, concentrated nuts or cubes, chaff, salt and mineral licks. Vitamin supplements can be given but one type only should be used to provide the extra vitamins your horse may need.

Hay is the main bulk and fibre feed for horses and should be given during day and night. It takes the place of grass which may not be freely available and helps the digestion of the horse. There are two main types of hay: seeds and meadow hay. Seeds hay is a hard, coarse hay, rich in protein and suitable for horses in fast work. Meadow hay is a softer hay with a higher water content which makes it more fattening and more easily digestible. It consists of many different grasses and weeds, such as dandelions and clovers. All hay should be sweet-smelling and should not be fed until it is approximately six months old, to ensure that there are no gases left from the drying process, which could cause colic (see page 114). If hay is really good, most grass-kept riding ponies can live very well on it alone, with an additional feed given only when the pony is doing extra work.

Bran is another bulk feed and is used with other foods to make the meal more palatable. Fed dry it is a binding food, fed wet it is a laxative. Once a week before the horse's day off, he should be given a bran mash with a tablespoon of Epsom salts. Because this is easily digestible, it is also a good feed for the sick horse (see pages 116-117). Bran mash is prepared by pouring boiling water over the bran. It is then covered with a cloth or sack and left to cool and steep before feeding. It may be flavoured with anything the horse likes, such as apples or a handful of oats. Bran mash also makes a very effective poultice for the foot, if it has sustained an injury.

Oats, because they are full of protein, are an energy-giving food, essential for horses doing really hard work. They are not usually recommended for horses or ponies who are not being worked too hard and may make ponies over-fresh and excitable.

Barley is a more fattening food and helps to maintain condition. It should be fed bruised or crushed, never whole, and in small quantities, as it swells the stomach. It can also be fed boiled with bran. It needs several hours' boiling and preferably left overnight.

Concentrated nuts or cubes are a commercially produced foodstuff, providing a balanced food containing essential quantities of protein and carbohydrates, plus vitamins and minerals. They are supplied in numerous different combinations, suitable for all animals, from ponies at grass to supremely fit race horses. Horse and pony nuts are ideal for the general riding horse or pony.

Chaff is chopped hay sometimes mixed with oat straw and is useful for giving extra bulk to the feed. It also prevents a greedy horse from bolting or eating his feed too fast.

Salt encourages the horse to drink which stimulates the kidneys and helps to keep the digestive system in good, working order, so that full benefit is derived from the food. A handful of cooking salt can either be given in one feed a day or a salt lick (which is a block of salt) can be placed in the manger.

▲ Hay, bran, salt, oats and concentrated nuts are the basic feeding requirements to keep a horse in good condition. Together with water, which aids the digestion, they provide all the protein, carbohydrate, fibre, salt and vitamins essential for a well balanced diet

▲ Hay for the stabled horse should be provided either in a hayrack which is fixed to the wall, or in a haynet as shown in the photograph. It must be tied securely and placed fairly high up, so that as it empties and drops there is no risk of the horse getting his foot caught in it

Minerals are necessary only if they are deficient in the horse's diet, for instance if he is at grass on poor pasture. They can be given in the form of a lick, which should be placed in a container in the horse's field. Most concentrated feed includes adequate amounts of minerals.

The type and amount of food given to a horse depends largely on the amount of work he is doing and the following charts give a rough guide to feeding three horses in different situations.

A pony at grass, hunting and being ridden in Pony Club activities during the winter

8a.m.	1kg (2lb) horse and pony nuts
5p.m.	1kg (2lb) horse and pony nuts
	Small haynet

A horse out in a New Zealand rug at night and in during the day, being ridden daily and competing in Riding Club activities

8a.m.	1kg (2lb) horse and pony nuts
	Small haynet after exercise
12.30p.m.	1kg (2lb) horse and pony nuts. Hay
5p.m.	1kg (2lb) horse and pony or stud nuts
	½kg (1lb) bran with a double handful of chaff. Carrots

A stabled horse being ridden daily and turned out for a few hours three or four times a week

8a.m.	1kg (2lb) horse and pony nuts
	Haynet after exercise
12.30p.m.	1kg (2lb) horse and pony nuts
	1kg (2lb) bruised barley. Hay
5p.m.	1kg (2lb) horse and pony or stud nuts
	½kg (1lb) bran with chaff and carrot or any other root vegetable. Hay
9p.m.	Hay for the night

International breeds

The horse has developed over millions of years. The many breeds in existence today were originally descended from numerous herds of small, wild horses that roamed the plains of the world. Over the centuries man tamed and domesticated the horse for his own use and later experimented with the breeding to produce horses suitable for different tasks and environmental conditions. Several different breeds emerged, each with its own characteristics.

The following photographs show just a few of the world's most famous breeds.

▲ The Thoroughbred can trace its history to three imported Arab stallions brought to England in the eighteenth century. Unequalled in speed, elegance and ability, it dominates racing and most equestrian sports worldwide

▲ The Norwegian Fjord Pony, said to have been bred and kept by the Vikings, stands about 1·42m (14 hands) high. He is dun in colour, extremely strong with a short, thick neck, highly intelligent and easily trained for work

▲ The Morgan, one of the most popular of the American breeds, was founded through one tough little stallion at the end of the eighteenth century. His stock all reproduced his hardiness, good looks and temperament

▲ The Arab from the Middle Eastern deserts is the most famous horse of all and has dominated breeding throughout the world. It is renowned for its exquisite head, flared nostrils, flowing mane and tail, intelligence and speed

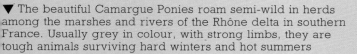

▼ The beautiful Camargue Ponies roam semi-wild in herds among the marshes and rivers of the Rhône delta in southern France. Usually grey in colour, with strong limbs, they are tough animals surviving hard winters and hot summers

▲ The Anglo-Arab is a cross between a Thoroughbred and Arab. This mare shows the fine qualities of both breeds and her foal, a French Thoroughbred/Dutch Grönigen cross, possesses the characteristics of a potential dressage horse

▲ The Trakehner is an ancient and much sought after German breed, renowned for its endurance and courage. Originally a heavier type, it was crossed with Thoroughbreds and today the breed is strong but light and versatile

Day-to-day care

The healthy horse

When you own a horse, it is vital that you devote as much time as you can to his health and welfare. Sadly, one too often sees animals in an appalling state, not necessarily through lack of care but through ignorance and unawareness.

If your pony is at grass, he will need adequate land, well fenced so that it is safe, with good pasture, a continuous water supply and some form of shelter to protect him from the sun and flies in summer, and the wind and rain in winter. This information is covered in detail on page 88.

If you have a stabled horse (see pages 90-91), he must be kept warm in a box that has no draughts. There must be good drainage, pure air circulation, a clean, dry floor with adequate bedding, good light and plenty of water and food.

A healthy looking horse is a pleasure to have. He should be alert and happy and have a nice, glossy coat if stabled, well rounded quarters and plenty of flesh all over, yet not be too fat. A horse in poor condition will have ribs showing because he is too thin, a poor looking neck, angular quarters, a harsh, staring coat, pot belly and dull eyes.

One of the main causes of a horse's loss of health is worms. A worm infestation can cause great damage to all horses whether stabled or at grass and for this reason control of worms is one of the most vital elements in good horse management. Regular worming should be carried out every six to eight weeks, and the type of dose varied, as worms tend to become immune to one variety. Consult your veterinary surgeon about worming. He will advise on the types of worm dose and probably leave you a few months' supply. The dose is usually administered with a special worming gun, like a syringe, which ensures the correct amount is given, and the diagram shows how this is done.

There are various types of worm which affect horses. Bots, the larvae of the gadfly, lay their eggs during late summer and autumn on the horse's skin. When they hatch, the horse licks them off and they eventually reach his stomach. In small numbers they can be fairly harmless but in large quantities they cause a lot of damage.

Round worm is common and in large quantities causes loss of condition and intermittent colic.

The most dangerous of all is the red worm, so named because of the blood it sucks. In larvae-form it may damage blood vessels and other organs. Young horses especially are very severely affected by this type of infestation, the symptoms of which are loss of condition, anaemia and irregular bowel movements. A horse that has

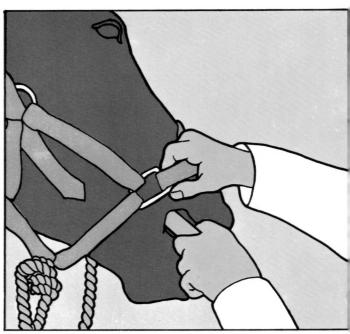

▲ Regular worming every six to eight weeks is a vital element in good horse management, as a worm infestation is one of the major causes of a horse's loss of health and condition. The dose can be administered by the vet or the horse's owner and a special worming gun, like a syringe, is used, which ensures that the correct amount is given

had a severe infestation of red worm may never fully recover.

Healthy teeth are important, for if a horse cannot chew his food properly, he will lose condition. A horse's teeth should be rasped once or twice a year by the veterinary surgeon, or by a horse dentist if there is one locally. Look out constantly for indications of bad teeth. If the horse is chewing in an unhappy way, it may be because his teeth are so sharp that with every bite he is cutting the inside of his mouth. If he holds his head to one side when chewing, it may be that he has a decaying tooth. Loss of appetite and condition, if not due to worms, may well be due to teeth problems.

Most vets will recommend tetanus protection and also protection against the many types of equine flu. There are now several brands combining the two vaccinations. It is a good idea to book your vet to come to look at your horse on a regular basis, so that he can inspect the teeth, carry out flu and tetanus vaccinations and possibly a worm count at the same time. Most flu vaccinations are best given when the horse can have a few easy days afterwards.

Cared for in this way, together with constant vigilance by you for any signs of abnormality, your horse should lead a happy, healthy life.

Clipping and trimming

A horse will normally change his coat twice a year. He will grow a thicker coat for the winter and shed it for a finer one for the summer. If he is at grass during the winter, his thick coat and the extra greasiness underneath it will keep him reasonably warm. However, if he is stabled, the extra thick coat may become a nuisance if he sweats profusely, and in this case, the horse should be clipped.

Clipping helps a horse's condition by enabling him to work without sweating and therefore to work harder, to dry off quickly after he has been working and to stay clean. A horse is usually clipped two or three times from late autumn to early winter and once in mid winter. He should then be left until he starts to change his coat naturally. At this stage extra grooming and hand massage will help to remove the loose coat.

There are four standard types of clip, three of which are illustrated on the right, and the type you choose depends largely on the amount of work the horse is doing. As clipping is a fairly specialized job, it needs a great deal of practice to perfect and you may prefer to have this professionally done, for which the cost is relatively low.

Electric clippers are by far the most satisfactory type to use and although they make rather a loud, buzzing noise, the horse will soon get used to it and settle down. Make sure the blades of the clippers are sharp before you start.

Keep an even pressure on the skin as you clip, working in long lines against the lie of the coat. Wipe the blades periodically with a little paraffin oil and brush them to get rid of the hairs. Be very gentle when clipping the legs and head and take care not to cut the mane and tail.

The clippers can also be used to trim and tidy the jaw line and the heels. The effect should be even with no ridges or lines. The area just behind the ears can be clipped to allow the bridle to rest on it comfortably.

Clippers or scissors can be used to straighten the end of the tail. Rest the tail over an assistant's arm, then cut it to a length of approximately 10cm (4in) below the point of the hock. Pulling the top part of the tail takes several days, as only a few hairs at a time should be taken. Pull the hairs from the sides, then put on a tail bandage daily to keep the tail neat. Full tails should be left at the top and simply straightened at the bottom.

To trim the mane, pull a few hairs out at a time from underneath, with the help of a mane comb (see page 100). Once the mane has been thinned, pluck the ends by hand to make them even.

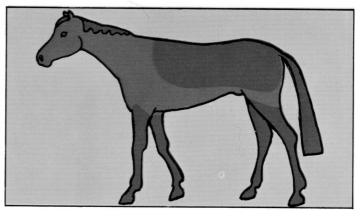

▲ The blanket clip: the head, neck and belly are clipped out, leaving a patch in the shape of a blanket. This type of clip is used on a stabled horse that sweats heavily and is not involved in very serious work

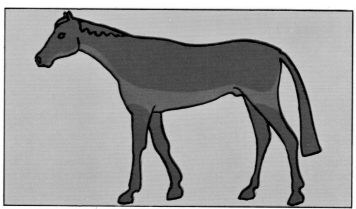

▲ The trace clip: the hair is clipped from the belly, under the neck and up the back of the quarters. This is ideal for the stabled horse doing light work or for the horse or pony at grass wearing a New Zealand rug (see pages 102-103)

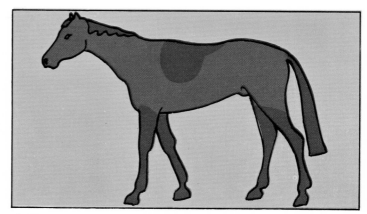

▲ The hunter clip: only the legs and a saddle patch are left unclipped. This is for the stabled horse in hard work, the unclipped legs giving protection against knocks, scratches or bruises. If the horse is involved in racing or advanced competition work, he can be clipped out completely

The foot

The rider has approached the horse quietly and patted him before starting to run her hand from the top of the leg downwards

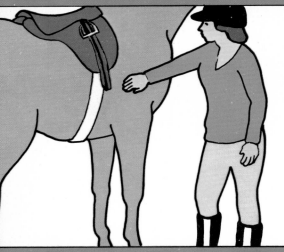
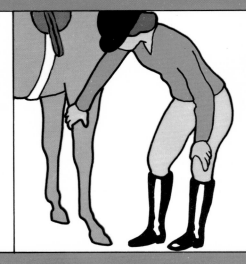
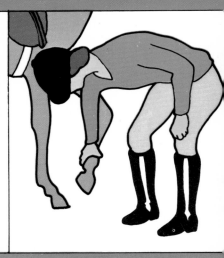

The leg has been caught hold of near the foot without any warning and the horse may kick out or shoot forward in fright

▲ Picking up a horse's foot is an easy exercise, so long as it is carried out smoothly and quietly. The rider is going to inspect one of the front feet, so she approaches the horse quietly towards his shoulder. She places her hand at the top of the leg

▲ She then runs her hand gently down the leg towards the fetlock joint. If at this stage the horse does not automatically start to lift his leg, the rider should exert a little pressure on it and pull it gently up

▲ The horse has lifted his leg and the rider has slipped her right hand down on to the foot. She will then bring her other hand over to support the foot while she first inspects it thoroughly for any signs of abnormality, then uses the hoof pick to clean it out

The saying 'No foot, no horse' alone explains the importance of proper care of the feet. They should be checked thoroughly every day for any signs of abnormality, and picked out with a hoof pick (see pages 100-101). Except in cold weather they should be washed at least three or four times a week, dried well and hoof oil applied.

Special care should be given to feet with thin soles. The horse should be stabled on good, dry bedding and the feet hardened by soaking them for ten minutes daily in salt and water.

The shoes should also be checked daily to see they are fitting correctly. Horses should be shod every four to six weeks. Unshod horses should have their feet rasped by the blacksmith at regular intervals, to prevent cracks developing.

The rider has lifted the horse's leg gently and is about to ▶ bring her other hand down to support the foot while she inspects it. The blacksmith nailing on a hind shoe, opposite, is surrounded by the tools of his trade: rasps, pinchers, a paring knife, hammer and anvil

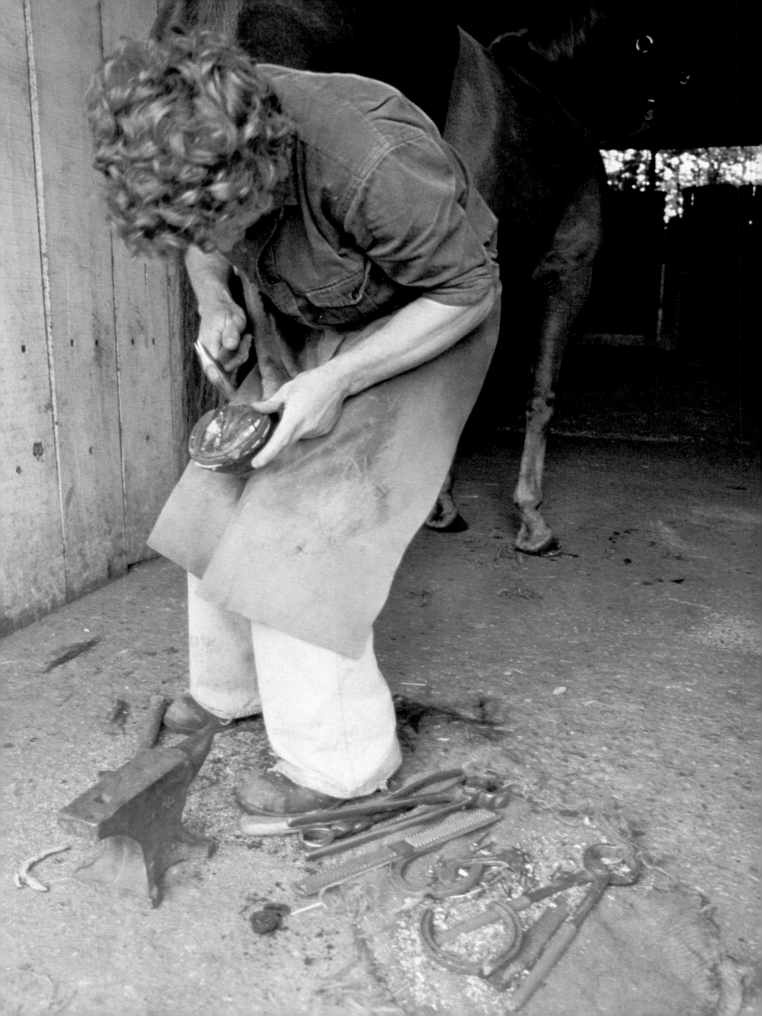

Grooming

These are the essential items that make up your grooming kit. **1** The water brush for damping down the mane and tail, and for washing the feet **2** The dandy brush for removing heavy dirt and caked mud, particularly from the grass-kept pony **3** The body brush for removing dust, scurf and grease from the coat, mane and tail **4** The sweat scraper for removing excess sweat or water **5** The rubber curry comb for removing mud from an unclipped pony **6** The metal curry comb for cleaning the body brush **7** The mane and tail combs for untangling the mane and tail of a grass-kept pony, for pulling the mane and tail and for plaiting purposes **8** The hoof pick for cleaning out the foot and removing stones **9** The brush for applying the hoof oil **10** Hoof oil for keeping the foot healthy and free from cracks **11** The stable rubber for a final polish after grooming **12** The sponge for cleaning the eyes, nose and dock

Grooming is the necessary daily attention to the feet and coat of the stabled horse. It promotes health by stimulating the circulation, it improves the appearance by ensuring cleanliness and it maintains condition. The grass-kept horse or pony should not be groomed, as this removes the natural grease in the coat which keeps him warm. He should have the worst of the dirt brushed off, so that he looks respectable to ride.

The items you need to make up your grooming kit are described in the following paragraphs and illustrated above.

The body brush is for removing dust, scurf and grease from the coat, mane and tail. It should be cleaned with the metal curry comb. This type of comb should not be used on the horse but the rubber curry comb is useful for removing mud from an unclipped pony.

The dandy brush is for removing heavy dirt and caked mud, and is particularly useful for cleaning the grass-kept pony. It should not be used on the head, mane or tail, or on a clipped horse, as it is too hard.

The water brush, used wet, is for damping down the mane and tail to tidy their appearance, and for washing the feet. The sponge should be used for cleaning the eyes, nose and dock, and the stable rubber (similar to a teatowel) is used for a final polish after grooming.

The hoof pick is for cleaning out the foot and removing stones that become lodged, and is one of the most important grooming implements. Hoof oil is for keeping the foot healthy and free from cracks and should be applied with a brush.

The mane and tail combs can be used to help comb out the tangled mane and tail of a grass-kept pony but are generally used only for pulling the mane or tail and for plaiting purposes.

The sweat scraper is for removing excess sweat or water. It should be used gently on tender and prominent parts and never used below the knees or hocks, or on the head.

Before the horse is groomed, he should be tied up securely and the grooming kit placed within easy reach. The body brush should be used first with firm, sweeping, circular strokes in the direction of the lie of the coat, working from the top of the neck towards the tail, as shown in the photograph. A dandy brush should not be used on this type of horse, as it is too hard for his fine skin. After about every half a dozen strokes, the brush should be cleaned by drawing it smartly across the metal curry comb and tapping out the dirt. Once the coat is thoroughly groomed on one side, the inside and outside of the legs should be brushed and then the same process repeated on the horse's other side. Ticklish spots, particularly under the tummy, should be rubbed gently with the hand and the stable rubber to remove the dirt.

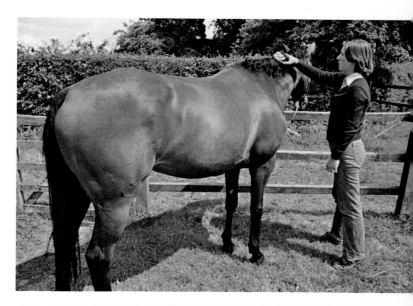

The head should be brushed gently with the body brush. The head collar can be slipped round the horse's neck while this is being done and a hand should be placed on his nose to keep him steady. When brushing round the ears and under the jaw, special care must be taken not to knock any tender parts or bony projections. The photograph shows the sponge being used to wipe the eyes. It should then be used to wipe the nose and nostrils, the dock and under the tail, in that order. A bucket of water is needed in which to rinse the sponge after each area has been cleaned and also to wet the water brush which is used to dampen – or 'lay' – the mane and tail. This encourages the hairs to lie in the same direction and so make the mane and tail look neat and tidy.

The feet should then be attended to. They should be inspected thoroughly and carefully picked out with the hoof pick, starting from the heel and working towards the toe. The cleft of the frog should be cleared and a check made that the shoes are secure. The feet should be washed at least three or four times a week, except in very cold weather when there is a risk of the heels cracking. The heels must be dried carefully and petroleum jelly applied if they show any signs of soreness. The feet should then be oiled inside and out. If the tail is very tangled, the hairs should be separated by hand and about once a week brushed out with the body brush, as shown in the photograph. A tail bandage should be put on to keep the tail neat. The horse should be given a final dusting over with the stable rubber, then put back in the stable and rugged up.

Rugs and blankets

Except in very warm climates a stabled horse needs a rug of some sort throughout the year. There are many types from which to choose but the most essential are a day rug, a night rug, a summer sheet and possibly a blanket for the winter months. A roller, made of leather or webbing, is needed to keep the rugs in place, although some rugs are designed with straps for this purpose. A wither pad, usually made of sheepskin or sacking, should be worn with a roller to prevent it from causing pressure sores.

Day rugs are made of a thick, woollen material, braided round the edge and are used for warmth in the stable during the day. If the weather is very cold at night, the day rug can be put on under the night rug for additional warmth but care must be taken to ensure that the two rugs do not cause pressure on the withers.

Night rugs are usually made of hemp or jute and lined with a woollen material. They are sometimes provided with a surcingle (a canvas strap) which keeps the rug in place but its use is not recommended, as it causes pressure on the backbone. The roller should be used for this purpose. Night rugs are subject to considerable soiling when the horse lies down, so it is advisable to buy a fairly cheap one. If you do not want to go to the expense of buying a night rug at all, use the day rug placed inside out on the horse at night, then in the morning shake it out and place it the right way round.

Summer sheets are made of cotton and are usually coloured or checked and braided. They are used when it is too hot for woollen rugs and to help to keep the horse clean and protected from flies. As they are easily washable, it is practical to put them on under day or night rugs, as they help to keep these clean.

Blankets are usually made of a heavy, woollen material and are often yellow with coloured stripes. They are put on under a rug for extra warmth in cold weather. A household blanket is perfectly adequate for this purpose.

Anti-sweat sheets, made of open cotton mesh, are useful when the horse is hot, for instance after a competition, as they allow the air to circulate through the mesh but still give some warmth. Once the horse is dry, a rug should be put on for additional warmth. A cheaper way of producing the same effect is to sprinkle straw liberally along the horse's spine, then cover it with a light sheet or hessian sack and secure it with a roller. It is dangerous to leave a hot or cold sweating horse in a stable in case he catches a chill. If he is brought back to the stable still wet, he should be turned out immediately to dry himself off by walking about or having a roll.

New Zealand rugs, made of canvas lined with wool, are designed for horses turned out in the winter and should not be worn in the stable. They are waterproof, to provide protection against wind, rain and snow, and have special leg straps which prevent the rug falling off when the horse lies down to roll. Some New Zealand rugs also have a roller surcingle already attached to keep them in place. It is important to get your horse used to this type of rug before turning him out in it, as the stiffness of the canvas and the feel of the leg straps may upset him at first. Keep the leg straps well oiled, as they tend to rub sensitive horses and check the withers and shoulders daily for soreness from pressure. A wither pad sewn inside the rug usually solves the problem of rubbing.

Rugs should be used sensibly, according to the weather and the type of horse. Unclipped and fine-skinned horses need the warmth provided by rugs but little ponies with long, shaggy coats may probably never need them. Remember that the temperature drops considerably at night, so rug up accordingly. A simple way of finding out whether your horse is cold is by feeling his ears. If they are cold, then he is, so rug him up and rub his ears gently to help to warm him.

The anti-sweat sheet is used when the horse is hot or wet ▶ after work, as the open cotton mesh allows the air to circulate while still providing warmth. As soon as the horse is dry, a rug should be added. The sheet can also be used under a day or night rug to provide additional warmth

▼ The horse blanket, made of a heavy woollen material and traditionally yellow with stripes, is put on under a rug for extra warmth in cold weather. The photograph shows how the blanket is put on with the corners folded back. The rug is then placed on top and the top point lapped over it

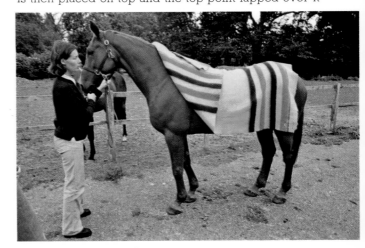

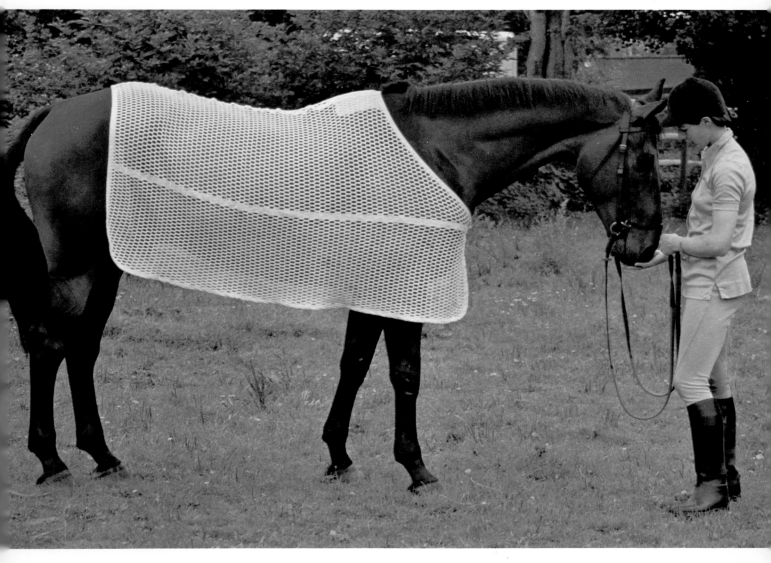

▼ The night rug, made of jute, has now been placed on top and the point of the blanket folded back over it. This helps to keep the blanket in place and prevent it from slipping back as the horse moves. A roller made of leather keeps both the blanket and rug secure

▼ The New Zealand rug, made of waterproof canvas lined with wool, is designed to protect horses turned out in winter from wind, rain and snow. The surcingle roller and special leg straps, which are being fastened, keep the rug in place and prevent it from falling off when the horse rolls

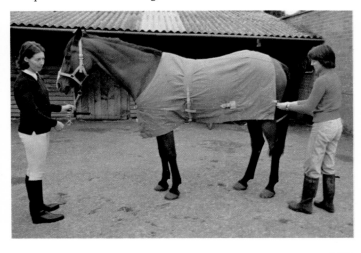

Day-to-day care
Care of tack

▲ Tack should be cleaned regularly if it is to be maintained in good condition. These two are cleaning their tack outside with sponges, water and saddle soap which is set in a home-made block of wood, for easy handling

Your tack is one of the most expensive items concerned with riding but if it is stored properly and cleaned regularly, it should last a lifetime. Bridles should be hung on hooks placed either in the wall or ceiling, as shown in the photograph on page 24, and saddles should be stored either on saddle racks, as shown in the photograph on the opposite page, or on a saddle horse which is a piece of apparatus, usually made of wood, on which the saddle rests safely without slipping. All tack should be carefully inspected from time to time and special attention paid to the stitching and buckles which may become loose with wear.

To clean your tack you need the following items: a tin or bar of plain or glycerine saddle soap, available from a saddler; a sponge for applying the saddle soap; a rough sponge or piece of towelling or sacking for wiping, washing and rinsing; a tin of metal polish; stable rubbers or cloths for applying and cleaning off the metal polish; an old dandy brush.

The bridle should be cleaned when necessary but periodically it should be given a thorough washing. It should be completely dismantled and every piece washed with warm water and saddle soap. The bit needs special attention, as it becomes covered with grass which when dry is

difficult to remove. It is therefore advisable to rinse the bit in water as soon as it is taken off the horse. Once the bridle is washed, all metalwork should be dried carefully and polished with metal polish. The bridle should then be reassembled. The reins should be slipped through the throat lash which should then be fastened, and the nose band placed round the outside of the bridle.

Head collars, halters, rollers and rug buckles should be cleaned regularly and the metal polished.

For daily cleaning care, the saddle should be placed on a saddle horse or fence and the girths, stirrup leathers and irons removed. The top of the saddle should be wiped with a well dampened and wrung out sponge or piece of towelling. Black grease marks, known as jockeys, should be removed with a piece of towelling.

The saddle should then be soaped, using a slightly dampened sponge rubbed well in saddle soap. If the lining is made of linen, this should simply be wiped with a damp sponge and then

▲ Care of tack also includes proper storing. Saddles should be kept on racks and other equipment, such as bridles, stirrup leathers and head collars, should be hung on hooks. The wooden piece of apparatus is a specially designed stand for easy cleaning of the underside of saddles

This saddle has been correctly laid on the ground, ▶ resting on its front arch, with the stirrup irons run up and the girths placed across the seat. Whenever it is necessary to lay a saddle on the ground, it should be placed in this position and never laid on its back

the saddle should be stood on its front arch, as shown in the photograph on the right, and left to dry. Serge linings should be brushed with the dandy brush, then scrubbed with soap and water once a week. When the cleaning operation is over, the saddle should be placed on a rack and covered with a clean cloth or stable rubber.

If the girths are made of leather, they should be washed with soap. If they are made of string or nylon, they should be brushed well with the dandy brush. Alternatively, both types can be washed in mild detergent.

Irons and leathers should be washed with soap, dried and hung separately if they are used infrequently, or replaced on the saddle.

All tack that is not being used regularly should be cleaned well, smeared with petroleum jelly, then covered and kept dry. The petroleum jelly should be wiped off before the tack is used.

Special equipment

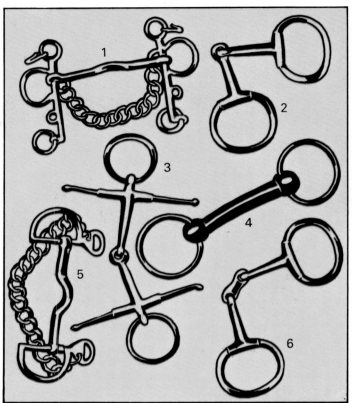

▲ The diagram shows six types of bit: **1** Pelham **2** Jointed egg-butt snaffle **3** Fulmer snaffle **4** Rubber snaffle **5** Kimblewick **6** Double-jointed snaffle. The snaffle bits are the mildest and are used for everyday riding; the pelham and kimblewick are used for when greater control is needed

▲ This impressive collection of bits gives some indication of the number and types available, each designed for a special purpose or situation. Some are old bits, some are new, some have a mild action on the horse's mouth and some are severe and suitable for use only by the experienced rider

▼ This police horse is immaculately turned out in his magnificent ceremonial bridle, highly polished for the occasion, with a reversible pelham bit. This is a variation of the pelham, shown in the diagram on the left, peculiar to the British Army and Police Force

Horses are born with sensitive mouths and in order to maintain them, it is important to use as mild a bit as possible.

The mildest type of bit is the snaffle, of which there are many types and some are shown in the diagram above. This is a straight or jointed single bit usually made of rubber, vulcanite or metal, with rings at either end to which the cheek pieces and reins are attached. The most popular and widely used type of snaffle is the jointed egg-butt, as it has rounded ends which do not pinch the corners of the horse's mouth.

The two bits of a double bridle are used by a knowledgeable rider to produce sophisticated results from a well schooled horse. Both bits have cheek pieces and reins attached to them (see the diagram on page 24). One bit is a narrow version of the snaffle, called a bridoon. The second bit has a chain and is called a curb.

The pelham and kimblewick bits are combinations of the snaffle and curb bits. They have a single curb bit to which two reins are attached, and are used if greater control is needed than that provided by the snaffle.

Special equipment
Side-saddle

▲ The rider is seated side-saddle on her pony and has left off the skirt of her habit so that the leg position can be clearly seen. Her right leg is resting over one pommel and her left leg under the other pommel. Her back is straight and her hands are placed either side of the pony's withers

▲ Complete with skirt, the rider is now appropriately dressed for riding side-saddle. Adults would wear a bowler hat with veil instead of the hunting cap. The rider's far hand is holding a stick which she will use to replace the guide normally given by the leg on the pony's offside

From the back the rider must be seen to be sitting absolutely straight in the saddle at all times. If she allows herself to slip to one side, she will throw both herself and her pony out of balance and will have to cling on to the pommels in an effort to retrieve her position ▶

Riding side-saddle is a most elegant sight and is once again increasing in popularity. Once you have mastered this style of riding, you will be able to have great fun competing in the Ladies Side-saddle Classes.

Learning to ride side-saddle is not difficult but it is not easy to do it well. The secret of success is to remain sitting straight on the horse and not to let yourself slip to one side, so that you have to cling on to the pommels to retrieve your position and balance.

When you are seated side-saddle, both legs should lie on one side of the horse, usually the left. The right leg should rest over one pommel and the left one under the other pommel. The hands should be kept low on either side of the withers, and a longish stick or whip should be carried to replace the guide normally given by the leg on the horse's offside.

When you are competing in side-saddle classes, you should wear a habit, which consists of a specially designed skirt and coat, with a collar and tie. Children should wear this with a hunting cap, adults with a bowler hat and veil.

▲ This simple, split-eared bridle is the most popular type of the many varieties in use. The loop over the ear keeps the bridle firmly in place and allows it to be put on the horse quickly and easily. The partly braided mane is suitable for competing in a Western Riding Class

◄ This is a rather old-fashioned but typical Western saddle, with a high cantle and leather stirrups, one of which can be seen laid across the seat. As it has two girths – called cinches – it is known as a double-rigged saddle, the back cinch being used when roping to keep the saddle in place

▼ Western saddles are tremendously strong, as they have to take the weight of steers which are roped to the high pommel which is called a horn. This saddle is a more modern type than the one shown on the left and because it is so beautifully decorated, it is ideal for showing purposes

▲ This typically dressed cowboy shows the position of the Western-style rider. The reins are held in one hand above the horn of the saddle, leaving the other hand free for roping, the legs are almost straight and the feet are resting comfortably in the leather-covered stirrups

Western riding has increased tremendously in popularity all over the world. It has now become a leisure sport for thousands and big business for breeders of horses for Western riding.

In ranching countries the cow-horse is part of the way of life. It is bred and trained to pick out steers and herd cattle as a sheepdog herds sheep. The horses bred for this purpose are extremely fast and powerful. They are usually called cutting horses and are used extensively in the United States, South America and Australia.

Western saddles are designed for comfort and use when roping. They are often lavishly decorated, as shown in the photograph opposite, and are tremendously strong, as they have to take the weight of steers and sometimes logs which are roped to the raised pommel, called a horn. The weight of the saddle is spread over a larger area than the British saddle and blankets are put on underneath it to prevent it from causing saddle sores during the long hours the horse is ridden.

When riding Western-style, the rider holds the reins in one hand and sits with his legs almost straight, resting comfortably in the stirrups.

▼ The wide stirrup leathers on this double-rigged Western saddle are designed for the rider's comfort. The rugs underneath protect the horse's back from sores and the coloured strap across the horse's chest is a Western breastplate which prevents the saddle from slipping back

Racing – the money spinner

Racing – 'the sport of kings' and spice of life to thousands – is perhaps the most exciting of all equestrian activities.

Nothing is more thrilling for the spectator than to watch good horses race past the finishing post, giving everything they have to earn that prized position in the winner's enclosure. Whether it was Mill Reef, The Minstrel, Brigadier Gerard, Bruni or Grundy, or from the United States, Seattle Slew, Secretariat or Aldyar, no one who has seen a great victory will ever forget it. Nor will they cease to marvel at the skill and energy of such jockeys as Lester Piggott, perhaps the world's greatest ever big race jockey, Willie Carson, Brian Fletcher, Greville Starkey, Pat Eddery, and from the States, young Steve Cauthen and Willie Shoemaker, the pocket Hercules. And who could fail to shed a tear as the great Red Rum battled home to win his legendary third Grand National.

▼ The legendary Red Rum, winner of three Grand Nationals, heads a string of race horses in the surf on Southport beach

▲ Willie Shoemaker from the United States, seen here on Hawaiian Sand, has won more races than any other jockey

▼ Lester Piggott, perhaps the world's greatest ever big race jockey, on Bruni, just ahead of Pat Eddery on Grundy

▲ Steve Cauthen from the States broke racing records by winning the greatest number of races as an apprentice jockey

▲ Lester Piggott and The Minstrel battle home to win the 1977 Derby, from Willie Carson on Hot Grove

Coping with ailments

Lameness is shown by a continuous unevenness of pace on level ground and it is essential to be able to recognize it, as further work with the horse could increase the severity of the injury.

To ascertain the affected leg, the horse should be led on a loose rein and walked or trotted past the vet or observer. The horse will put the weight on to his sound limb and nod his head as the sound leg touches the ground. The opposite leg will therefore be the injured one, although there are obviously a few exceptions.

The foot is the most common site of lameness, so it should be inspected first for any signs of the following causes or conditions:

Stones or sharp objects: these are the invariable cause of sudden lameness. A large object wedged between the shoe and the frog will be easily seen and can be removed with the hoof pick. Smaller ones may be less obvious, as they may have lodged deep in the cleft or at the side of the frog. Their removal will usually relieve lameness. If the horse is still lame, however, bruising may have occurred which will appear either as a red area or be simply tender to pressure. This should be treated either by applying a bran poultice, made in the same way as bran mash (see page 92), and leaving it on for twenty-four hours or by tubbing the foot, which involves cleaning it, then placing it in a bucket half full of warm water to which salt has been added. This should be done for half an hour twice daily and more warm water added as the water in the bucket cools.

Corns: these are bruises caused by pressure from a badly fitting shoe or neglect in having the horse regularly reshod. The part generally affected is just beneath the ends of the shoe near the heel. The shoe should be removed and the bruised part cut out by the vet. The foot should then be tubbed twice daily until the horse is sound, when the shoe can be replaced.

Sandcracks: these are vertical splits in the hoof which may occur because the horse has brittle feet or may be the result of an injury or continuous work on hard ground. They are painful if they become infected. In mild cases the blacksmith should be consulted but if they are causing lameness the vet should be called.

Laminitis: this is a painful inflammation of the sensitive inner structures of the foot. It affects both front feet or all four at a time and never a single foot. Its exact cause is unknown but it is

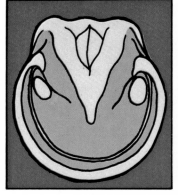
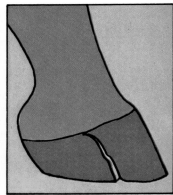
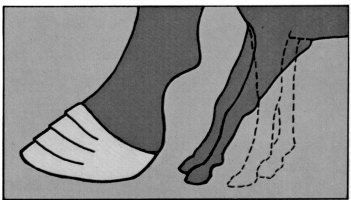

▲ These three conditions of the foot are common causes of lameness. The top two diagrams show corns, which are bruises in the sole of the foot, and a sandcrack, which is a vertical split in the hoof. The lower diagram shows the typical leg posture of a pony suffering from laminitis – the dotted lines indicate the normal stance – and the ringed effect on the hoof which may develop following a bad attack

▼ Cold hosing is excellent first aid treatment for all cuts and bruises, and will also help to cool the inflamed feet of a pony suffering from laminitis. The heels should always be dried thoroughly afterwards and petroleum jelly applied to prevent soreness and cracks

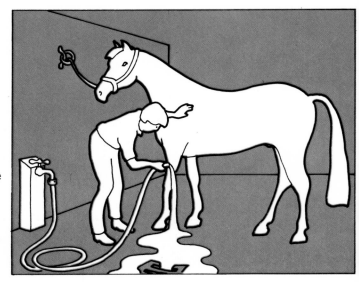

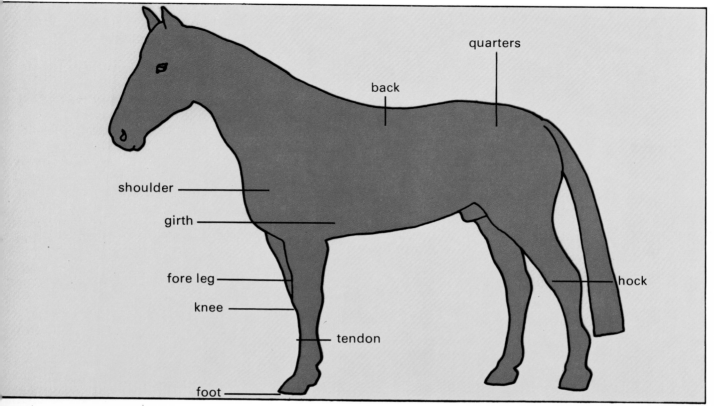

shoulder

girth

fore leg

knee

tendon

foot

back

quarters

hock

associated with ponies eating rich, spring grass. Badly affected ponies put all the weight on their heels and thrust their feet forward, and are in such pain that they are virtually impossible to move. The vet should be called and a strict, laxative diet of bran mashes (see page 92) given twice daily. The feet should be cooled by cold hosing and the pony encouraged to move to help the circulation. A ringed effect may develop on the hooves following a bad attack.

Thrush: this is a foul-smelling condition of the frog caused by wet bedding and general neglect of daily foot care. A badly affected area should be cut out and the frog cleaned and sprayed with antibiotic wound spray.

Seedy toe: this is similar to thrush but it affects the toe and is less serious. The treatment is the same as for thrush.

Another common site of lameness is the leg, particularly from the knee downwards. Problems in the leg include the following:

Splints: these are small, bony enlargements which may appear on the insides of the splint or cannon bones. They usually occur in horses under six years old and can be painful when

▲ The diagram shows the sites of lameness. The most common site is the foot which can be injured by stones or affected by such conditions as corns, sandcracks, laminitis, thrush and seedy toe. Lameness can also be caused by splints on the inside of the splint or cannon bones, sprains or strains in the tendon and hock, knocks to the knee and muscular injuries to the shoulder, back, girth and quarters

forming. If they cause lameness the horse should be rested until he is sound. Once the splints are formed, they usually remain and rarely cause any more trouble.

Sprains and strains: these occur most commonly in the tendons running down the back of the cannon bone but can also occur in the hock. Heat and swelling at the site of the injury are the first signs. Firm bandaging will give support and rest is the best cure but the vet should be consulted.

Wounds and cuts: if treated properly (see the following page), these should not cause too much trouble, so long as slow work is adopted until they have healed.

Lameness can also be caused by knocks to the knee joint and muscular injuries to the shoulder, back, girth and quarters. None of these causes is easy to diagnose and if your horse remains lame for no apparent reason, the vet should be called.

Coping with ailments
Elementary first aid

A first aid cupboard is essential in every stable. You should read the labels of the contents so that you know what they are for and how they are to be used. The name and telephone number of your local veterinary surgeon should be prominently displayed both on the cupboard and by the telephone. A suggested list of first aid contents is as follows:

> antiseptic solution, disinfectant and hydrogen peroxide, for cleaning wounds
> antibiotic wound powder or spray, for applying to simple cuts
> cotton wool and bowl, for bathing purposes
> medicated poultices and dressings
> gamgee tissue, to cover and protect dressings under bandages
> bandages, to hold dressings in place
> scissors, to cut dressings, etc
> kaolin and polythene, for poulticing bruises
> stub-ended thermometer
> salt, for adding to a bran poultice and for cleaning wounds
> Stockholm tar, for foot injuries
> petroleum jelly, for use with the thermometer
> cough electuary, for coughs .
> colic drench, for treating attacks of colic
> methylated spirit, for sore backs.

When you call your vet in an emergency, keep calm and describe the problem as clearly and as simply as you can. The type of questions the vet will want answered are as follows. If there is bleeding, is it severe, involving an artery or large vein, or a fairly simple tear which may require stitching, or is it a puncture wound? Has your horse got colic or is he showing similar symptoms of discomfort? Has he got a temperature and if so, what is it? Has he any discharge from his nose and if so, what colour is it? Has he any swelling round his head or throat? Is he lame and if so, is it an obvious foot problem or is there heat and swelling down his tendons?

Answers to this type of question will help the vet enormously to make an initial diagnosis and ascertain whether the problem is an emergency. Continuous bleeding is always an emergency, as is any case when the horse is in obvious pain.

The golden rule of first aid is to act quickly and sensibly. For instance, if the horse has a severed artery, control the bleeding with a tight bandage first, then phone the vet. If you have to use a lotion on a wound, wash your hands first, as infection is a greater danger than the wound itself. Have an assistant to help to calm the horse,

as he will probably be restless, and keep him warm if you are treating him outside.

The following are some of the common problems with which you may have to cope.

Wounds and cuts: small cuts should be bathed with salt and water, hydrogen peroxide, antiseptic solution or mild disinfectant, then treated with antibiotic wound powder or spray. Larger wounds and cuts should be hosed gently, as shown in the diagram on page 112, starting with a trickle of water and gradually increasing the flow, so as not to frighten the patient. If the wound is not too serious, it can simply be dusted with wound powder. Consult your vet about the use of antibiotics to prevent the spread of infection and also whether tetanus protection is necessary. Puncture wounds must be dealt with by the vet.

If a vein or artery is injured so that blood spurts from the wound, a tourniquet or pad and tight bandage should be applied to the wound, then the vet called urgently. Firm pressure over any serious bleeding will reduce or stop it.

Any severe tears will benefit from hosing with cold water until professional help arrives.

Foot injuries: the foot should be tubbed in a bucket of warm water to which salt has been added (see page 112). Alternatively, a bran poultice, made in the same way as bran mash (see page 92), should be applied to the injury and left on for twenty-four hours.

When a hind foot treads on the heel of a front foot, this is known as an overreach and can cause a very sore cut. The heel should be hosed or bathed clean, and wound powder or spray applied. The foot and heel should then be dressed and bandaged.

Girth galls and sore backs: these are caused by friction or pressure from girths or badly fitting saddles. The affected area should be bathed with salt and water until the soreness has disappeared, then hardened with methylated spirit. The horse should not be ridden but should be turned out or lunged (see pages 72-73) for exercise. If the saddle is the cause of the soreness, it should be checked by the saddler.

Colic: this is the term used to describe a pain in the belly. A horse with colic will sweat and be restless. He will look at his belly, try to lie down, kick at himself and appear generally uncomfortable. Other signs of colic are abnormal droppings and loss of appetite.

Give the horse a colic drench from a narrow-necked bottle by raising his head high and pouring a little of the mixture at a time into the side of his mouth where there are no teeth. Gently rub the gullet to encourage swallowing and keep the head up, so that the mixture does not trickle out. Do not let the horse roll and risk injury or a twisted gut but keep him walking, however hard he may try to lie down. If there is no improvement within half an hour or the condition worsens, call the vet.

Poisoning: yew and ragwort are poisonous to horses. Yew can kill and ragwort produces a toxin which damages the liver. The horse may show signs of colic or look generally unwell (see the diagram on page 117). If you suspect poisoning, call the vet at once.

Strains and sprains: these occur in ligaments and tendons. A kaolin poultice will help to relieve the pain and the injury should then be bandaged for support. The vet should be consulted and the horse rested until the injury has healed.

Eye injuries: professional advice should always be sought for these. Bruising to the eye lid can be bathed gently to reduce the swelling with lukewarm normal saline (one teaspoon of salt to about $\frac{1}{2}$ litre or 1 pint of previously boiled water). A cold teabag applied to the bruised area will also help to reduce the swelling.

Azoturia: known also as Monday Morning Disease or Set Fast, this is a sudden stiffness that affects horses in their quarters, giving a severe cramp-like pain. The horse may be anxious, and may sweat and tremble. If you are riding when this happens, dismount, take off the saddle and cover the horse with a coat, or rug if possible. Movement can damage the muscles, so keep him quiet, and get transport home and veterinary advice. This condition is often associated with too much protein in the diet for the amount of work being done. Reduce the protein and give a bran mash (see page 92) at least once or twice a week.

Skin troubles: spots or scabs are usually due to minor injuries or insect bites and should be bathed with salt and water. Occasionally a horse may contract ringworm or a similar, highly contagious disease. Ringworm shows as a raised, ringed area in which the hair eventually falls out,

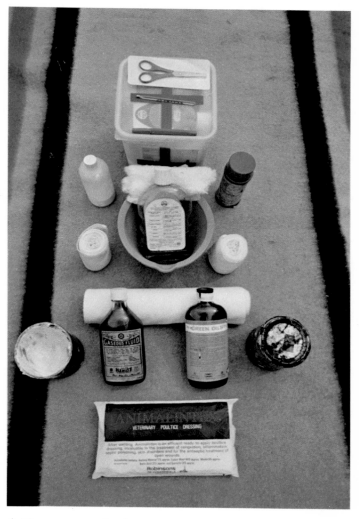

▲ The contents of a first aid cupboard: scissors and thermometer, wound powder and spray, small bowl with cotton wool and disinfectant, rolls of bandages and gamgee, tins of kaolin and Stockholm tar, colic drench, antiseptic solution for wounds and a packet of medicated poultices

leaving a raw, ringed patch. The vet should be consulted and the horse isolated. The use of grooming kit, rugs, saddle and bridle should be restricted to the affected horse, to prevent the disease from spreading. Once the horse has recovered, all articles including his box and your clothes should be disinfected.

Coughs and colds: there are at least four types of virus which may affect the nose, air passages and lungs, causing nasal discharge, glandular swelling and coughing. All except influenza (see the following page) produce mild symptoms only and recovery is usually complete within a week or ten days, provided the horse is rested. Take the horse's temperature and if it is 39°C (102°F) or over, consult the vet.

Coping with ailments
The sick horse

Before you can recognize a sick horse you need to know what constitutes a horse in healthy condition. He should be alert, which is shown by pricked ears and bright eyes. The skin should be loose and supple, the coat glossy and the body well covered with flesh. The droppings should be regular, and greenish or gold in colour, depending on the food he is eating. He should have a normal temperature, which for a horse is 38°C (100-101°F), his pulse rate should be 36-42 and his respiration rate 8-15. For a true reading, the temperature and pulse and respiration rates should be taken when the horse is at rest.

The sick horse will look lethargic and miserable, and his coat will be dull. He may hang his head and have his tail clamped in and ears back. His temperature and pulse and respiration rates may be raised. He may go through shivering attacks and have a thick, nasal discharge. He may also show signs of abdominal discomfort, such as kicking and looking at his stomach.

If your horse is showing any of these signs of sickness or discomfort, the first thing to do is to take his temperature. Shake the thermometer to ensure it is registering well below normal, then grease it with petroleum jelly. Raise the dock and gently insert the thermometer with a rotating action into the rectum. Keep hold of the end and leave it in this position for at least one minute, then remove it and take a reading. Any rise in temperature is abnormal, except, of course, immediately after exercise, and the vet should be called urgently if the thermometer registers 39°C (102°F) or over.

The pulse is usually taken where the facial artery passes under the jaw on either side, or at the median artery located in the centre of the inside of the fore leg. You will feel a regular pumping sensation at these spots and the beats should be counted for one minute.

The respiration rate is determined by watching the flanks as they move in and out with each breath and counting the movements for a minute. Alternatively, the rate can be taken by watching and counting the movements of the nostrils. The vet should be called if you notice any signs of respiratory distress.

Recording the horse's temperature on a chart and pinning it to the stable door is a useful way of seeing at a glance how the patient is progressing. Pulse and respiration rates can also be recorded in this way.

The most common ailments from which horses suffer today are equine flu and strangles, both of which require special attention.

The symptoms of equine flu, of which there are several forms, are similar to those shown in humans, and are usually a rise in temperature – though not in all cases – lethargy and nasal discharge. The horse may also cough, particularly if he is exerted. Vaccination against equine flu is now available and although not all viruses are yet covered, it certainly gives protection against a large number of them. It is usually wise to give the horse three or four easy days following vaccination, to allow him to recover fully from any side-effects.

Strangles is a highly infectious disease which most often affects young horses. Early symptoms are a high temperature, a cough and nasal discharge which is usually thick and yellow. A swelling between the upper jaw bones develops and turns into an abscess. Professional advice should be sought and the abscess bathed with hot water to which a tablespoon of Epsom salts is added. It is vital that the abscess is encouraged to open outwards, otherwise it will burst internally, and bathing is an effective way of drawing it to a head. Nasal discharge should be bathed away with warm, salty water.

With any illness, good nursing is of primary importance. The horse should be isolated if possible to help prevent the spread of infection. If this is not possible, restrict the use of any equipment to the affected horse and store it well away from other animals. Place a bucket of disinfectant outside the horse's box in which to rinse your hands when you have finished, and burn all dressings and swabs used on the horse.

If the horse is suffering from a respiratory infection, he will appreciate being able to hang his head over a half-door in his box. For nervous diseases or those affecting the eye, a darkened box is recommended.

The box should be well ventilated and free from draughts. Place extra straw or bales round the edges to keep it warm. The box should be clean at all times but if the horse is suffering from a cough, streaming nose or eye injury, be careful not to shake up the straw too much, as this creates dust. During mucking-out sessions, remove the horse to another box or arrange for someone to take him for a short walk.

Always keep your patient warm but avoid thick rugs and blankets and use a lighter form of clothing, as a weak horse will not be comfortable carrying any heavy weight. Stable bandages and gamgee will give additional warmth but these must be removed at night, and hand rubbing of

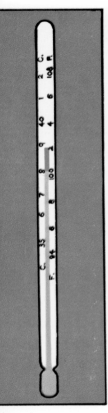

▲ This horse shows all the signs of sickness. His posture, with head hung low, ears back and tail clamped between the legs, indicates misery and lethargy. The thermometer, which shows a horse's normal temperature of 38°C (100-101°F), is registering 39°C (102°F), confirming that veterinary advice is required

he legs will help to restore poor circulation. Pulling the ears by taking hold of them at the poll and letting them slide gently through your closed hands will comfort and warm your horse.

During illness the horse's appetite will probably be extremely poor and this may well be an early sign that the horse is unwell. Let him eat as much as he feels well enough to cope with and do not try to force him to take more. Freshly cut green grass may be the most acceptable food but sliced apples or carrots may also be welcomed. Feed little and often, remove any stale feed from the box and make sure that all mangers or feed bins are kept scrupulously clean. Hay should be freely available and if the horse has a cough and running nose, it should be fed dampened, as this prevents irritation caused by dust.

Water is vital for the sick horse. Provide him with a constant supply and change it two or three times a day, so that it is always fresh.

All sick horses and those suddenly having to stop work for some reason should be kept on a daily laxative diet of bran mashes (see page 92) which keep the digestion working well when the stimulation of exercise is not possible. The mashes can be flavoured with any appetizing foods the horse will eat. At least one feed a day should have a handful of salt added if this is not

freely available in the stable. This encourages the horse to drink which aids digestion. If you are in any doubt about the way your horse is feeding, seek advice from your vet.

The sick horse should not be groomed but given a wipe over when his rug is removed and refreshed by sponging the eyes, nostrils and under the dock.

If the horse is very sick, you may have to stay with him constantly until he is over the worst stage. If this seems likely, arrange for someone to be easily available to call the vet or relieve you occasionally for a break.

Good nursing of sick animals is a matter of common sense and ensuring that all veterinary instructions are meticulously carried out. The aim is to relieve suffering and to provide the best possible care for a quick return to health. Most horses respond remarkably well to modern medications and with so many vaccines now available to prevent infectious diseases, it is becoming increasingly rare to see a really seriously sick horse.

Riding with caution

▲ It is essential that the rider knows the signals to use when on the roads and that they are made early and clearly. The rider is signalling here that she is going to turn to the left

▲ The rider is signalling that she is turning to the right. She should keep well into the side of the road until she actually makes the turn

▲ This signal is used when the rider is going to stop and wishes others to stay behind. When the way is clear, the rider should wave the traffic past

Riding on the road is perfectly safe if you have a docile horse who is quite unconcerned by the traffic, and the drivers are considerate. It can become a nightmare if you are on a nervous horse and the traffic is bad.

So be prepared before you go out. Make sure you are riding a horse you can control, that he is properly equipped and that you are wearing a hard hat. If you are riding at night have a stirrup light showing white to the front and red to the rear. Wear a fluorescent vest or armbands and a light-coloured jacket or sweater.

Always ride with both hands on the reins and have them at a sufficient length to keep your horse under control at all times. Know your highway code, ride in the same direction as the traffic, if possible on the grass verge, ride straight and do not allow your horse to wander.

Consideration to other road users is of paramount importance. Be aware at all times of drivers, walkers and cyclists. Look behind and in front of you before attempting to pass walkers or stationary objects and signal clearly before moving out. Any signal you make should be early and clear so that other road users are aware of your intentions. Allow sufficient room for the unexpected, such as car doors suddenly opening. Always warn vocally any person standing near a stationary vehicle, as sudden movements could upset the horse.

If you foresee trouble ahead of you, either make a detour or wait until the road is clear. Do not upset your horse on the road, as it is no place to teach him discipline.

When you are out for a ride in a group, make sure there are two experienced riders present, one to ride in front and one at the back. Never ride more than two abreast and if one of the horses in the group is fidgeting, arrange it so that he walks in front of others, as this will normally make him settle.

If you know your horse is not good on the road always make sure you ride with someone and have him ride on your outside or in front of you. Signal to the traffic to slow down if necessary, remembering to acknowledge the drivers with a smile and a thank you.

Avoid busy main roads if you can, as even the quietest horse can occasionally be frightened by very heavy traffic or huge juggernauts.

Before doing anything, remember to stop, look and listen and proceed only if it is safe to do so. Give way to pedestrians crossing and never take any risks on the roads. Walking is the safest pace but if you must trot, never do so around corners which are often slippery. If you are in difficulties, dismount and lead your horse.

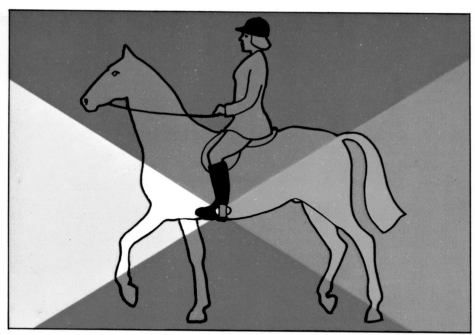

▲ The rider is slowing down and uses this signal to warn traffic behind her to do likewise. Riders should always acknowledge drivers with a smile and thank you when they show consideration

▲ When riding at night the rider wears a stirrup light showing white to the front and red to the rear. Here, she has the light on her left for riding where traffic drives on the right

▼ This group is riding sensibly on the side of the road, the youngest members between the more experienced. The rider at the back is warning the car behind to slow down

Safety at all times

The safety aspect of riding and owning a horse cannot be too strongly stressed and in most cases common sense and a few basic precautions are all that are needed to avoid accidents.

One of the first things to ensure when riding is that you have a correctly fitting, hard hat. It should be well padded inside and have a hard shell. To keep it firmly in place, a piece of elastic should be sewn on to it and fitted either under the hair at the back or under the chin. Alternatively, the hat can be worn with a safety harness, as shown in the photograph on the right. This is attached round the outside of the hat, taken under the chin and fastened securely.

In some countries the wearing of a hard hat is still not considered important but doctors throughout the world agree that the majority of serious head injuries from riding falls could have been avoided if the riders had been wearing a hard hat or had made sure that the hat they were wearing fitted securely.

Safety stirrup irons, shown in the photograph on the opposite page, are particularly useful for the beginner. They have a rubber band on the outside which breaks or slips off if the rider falls, so freeing the foot and preventing him from being dragged along the ground. Whatever type of iron is used, it must be the correct size for your foot: not so big that the foot can slip through, nor so small that the foot sticks in it. Stainless steel is the safest metal for irons. Pure nickel is not advisable, as it is soft and will bend or even snap.

Sensible shoes or boots should always be worn when riding. Jodhpur boots are the most suitable but a strong pair of walking shoes are adequate, especially in the early stages, so long as they have a heel which will prevent the foot from slipping through the iron and the sole is smooth.

Your tack must be safe to ride in, so check it regularly to see that the stitching is secure, the buckles in good order and particularly that the girths are strong and safe. Well cared for tack is unlikely to cause problems (see pages 104-105), but neglected tack could break and cause an accident. All tack should be stored sensibly. Bridles should be hung on hooks and saddles on racks, well out of harm's way. Any tack that is not being used regularly should be cleaned well, smeared with petroleum jelly, covered and kept dry. The tackroom should be locked at night.

If your horse is out at grass, make sure his field is safe. The fencing should be secure, with no broken rails, and particularly strong if the field is next to a road. Barbed wire is most

▲ Although the rider should always ensure that her hat fits securely, an added precaution is to wear a safety harness which keeps it firmly in place. This is attached round the outside of the hat and taken under the chin where it is adjusted so that the guard sits comfortably round the jaw

unsuitable for fencing, as it can cut the horse badly if he catches himself on it. Gates should shut securely and be fitted with padlocks if they open out on to a road.

Remove any dangerous objects in the field which the horse could tread on, such as jagged bits of wood or planks with nails in them. If harrows or any other pieces of agricultural equipment have to be left in the field, make sure they are well covered and protected from harming the horse. Dig out any poisonous plants such as yew, ragwort and rhododendron.

If you are turning two horses out together, make certain that they get on well together and if there is the slightest chance of their kicking each other, have their hind shoes removed first.

Remember that horses themselves can be dangerous. They are big, strong animals and become easily jealous. Take care if you have a bowl of food with you when you go to catch a horse that is out in the field with others, as they may all try to grab it at once, and do not take children or dogs into a field where there is more than one horse.

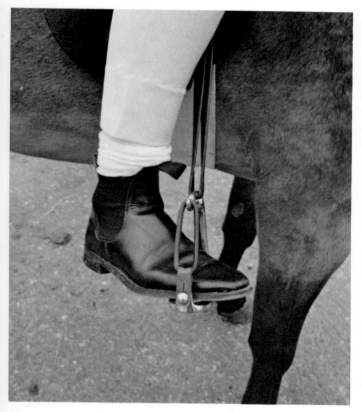

▲ The rider is sensibly equipped, wearing jodhpurs and jodhpur boots. The safety stirrup iron is particularly useful for the beginner, as the rubber band on the outside breaks or slips off if he falls, so freeing his foot and preventing him from being dragged along the ground

▲ If the rider gets into difficulties when trying to open a gate or is not confident of her own or her horse's ability to cope with it, she should dismount, run up her stirrup irons and lead the horse through, remembering to shut the gate securely behind her

If the horse is stabled, make sure that his box is absolutely safe, that there are no protruding nails in it and no sharp edges on mangers, water buckets and tops of doors. All door catches should be secure. Some horses can undo the top bolts, so it is advisable to have a bolt on the bottom of the door as well.

The haynet must be tied securely and fairly high up, so that as it empties and drops, there is no risk of the horse catching his foot in it.

Electrical fittings must be situated outside the horse's box and all wires tucked safely out of reach. There have been cases of horses being electrocuted on dangling wires inside the box. They must be inspected regularly, as faulty electrical fittings can cause fires.

Fire precautions are essential. Every stable should be equipped with fire extinguishers and easily accessible water. Never smoke in the vicinity of the stable, as, with so much hay and straw about, a smouldering cigarette end could quickly start a fire.

When children are concerned with horses, care should be taken. They should be taught from an early age not to stand directly in front or behind a horse. They should always be supervised when riding, particularly bareback when they may get into difficulties and need a helping hand to steady them.

Do not take any risks with your horse's health. He should be immunized yearly against equine flu and tetanus and wormed every six to eight weeks.

Be sensible when you are out riding. Do not attempt to ride on ground that looks boggy and do not jump anything you feel your horse is not competent to cope with. If you get into difficulties when trying to open a gate, or you are not confident of your own or your horse's ability to deal with it, dismount, run up your stirrup irons and lead your horse through, as shown in the diagram above, remembering to shut the gate securely behind you.

Insurance cover is important. Some equestrian federations (see page 123) run their own third party insurance schemes and can arrange many different kinds of insurance cover for yourself, your horse and your tack.

Ready for the off Now you can ride

By now you will not only have learned the techniques of the basic art of riding but have realized how much enjoyment there is to be gained from the sport. It is a sport which has so much to offer and one in which you can participate on so many levels.

It can be simply a weekend hobby when you ride at local stables or riding schools, or in the countryside where you can listen to the birds and watch the wild animals – they do not dash for cover as they would from someone on foot but accept a horse and its rider as one of themselves.

It can be a holiday pursuit that gives you two weeks' relaxation a year, when you go trekking in new parts of the country.

You may like to own a horse or pony, yet another aspect of the sport. This will bring you the enjoyment of being involved in the care of an animal that is dependent upon you for his welfare. You will discover the joy – and sometimes the frustration – a horse brings but above all, you will appreciate his willingness and companionship. Riding will become a very personal affair, as you will look upon your horse as a friend.

You may, however, see riding as a competitive sport and want the excitement and challenge of pitting your skills against others. In the world of competition there is so much to discover.

Before you enter a competition it is a good idea to find out as much as you can by going to events as a spectator. You will pick up tips, see the standard of riding required for each event and meet some of the people involved. Future events will be shown in your local newspaper or the equestrian magazines and when you come to competing, you should send for the schedule.

Never enter a competition that is of too high a standard for you. For instance, in Open Classes you may find yourself up against the professionals. Start with the Novice Classes for horses and riders, which are not too demanding and will give you initial experience. Do not enter with the sole idea of winning or your enjoyment will be ruined. Enjoy the preparation and the participation and treat the competition as a way of improving your standard of riding, furthering your experience and meeting new people. Winning is an added bonus and of course the sense of achievement is enormous, but it becomes important only when you have reached a very high standard.

The variety of activities associated with riding is enormous and whether you become involved at a competitive level or purely for relaxation is a matter of personal preference. That is the joy of riding – with so much to offer, it is a sport that appeals to people of all types and all ages.

Ready for the off
Further information

Your country's equestrian society or federation will always be willing to give help and advice on every aspect of horses and riding and the addresses of some of the major societies in America, Australia, Britain, Canada, Germany and New Zealand are given below.

Britain is probably the most highly horse-populated country in the world for its size and has many societies catering for every conceivable activity. Some of the major societies are described in detail as follows.

The British Horse Society promotes the interests of horse and pony breeding, furthers the art of riding and encourages horsemanship and the welfare of the horse. It is the parent body of the Pony Club and affiliated Riding Clubs.

It concerns itself with the conditions in which horses and ponies are kept, especially at sales and riding and horse-drawn caravan holiday centres. Through its training and examination system it has opened a professional career with horses. It also runs several courses for the enjoyment of riding at its base in Warwickshire.

A full member of the British Horse Society is automatically covered for third party legal liability insurance. The Society's insurers also offer members competitive insurance on all forms of horse activity and equipment.

The Society provides a special discount scheme which enables members to purchase a wide variety of goods at discount prices from a selection of shops. Members can also take advantage of the special facilities offered at many of the major equestrian functions.

The Pony Club has its headquarters at the British Equestrian Centre in Warwickshire. It started originally on a voluntary basis to encourage children in their riding. From this small beginning it has grown into one of the world's great youth movements and has now well over 1500 branches.

Membership of the Pony Club is open to anyone under the age of twenty-one and being a member provides one of the very best ways of furthering your knowledge of horsemanship and meeting people with similar interests.

The Pony Club runs a series of proficiency badges beginning at D standard and progressing to A which is a very high standard. These tests are conducted by qualified examiners and are universally recognized.

Several championships are held yearly following qualifying rounds in dressage, show jumping, horse trials and polo, and to compete in these or at Wembley for the Prince Philip Cup, the final for gymkhana games, is every child's dream come true.

The Riding Club is an adult version of the Pony Club and its branches are run in much the same way. They offer instruction in riding, organize visits to studs, hunt kennels and equestrian events and also run their own shows.

The National Pony Society looks after the interests of the Mountain and Moorland breeds of Britain, although each breed in turn also has its own society responsible for registering all pure-bred ponies and dealing with its own internal matters.

The following addresses may be useful in obtaining further information on equestrian matters or activities in various countries. Embassies can always give help on how to contact the horse society in their country.

GREAT BRITAIN
The British Horse Society, and the Pony Club, The British Equestrian Centre, Kenilworth, Warwickshire CV8 2LR.
The National Pony Society, 7 Cross and Pillory Lane, Alton, Hampshire.
Western Horseman's Association of Great Britain, 3 Church Style Cottage, Stoodleigh, Tiverton, Devon.
Ladies Side-saddle Association, 28 Featherbed Lane, Addington, Croydon, Surrey.
British Equestrian Insurance Brokers Ltd., Hildenbrook House, The Slade, Tonbridge, Kent.
AMERICA
United States Equestrian Team, Gladstone, N.J. 07934.
The American Horse Council, 1700 K Street, N.W., Washington D.C. 20006.
AUSTRALIA
The Equestrian Federation of Australia, c/o The Registrar, Showgrounds, Epsom Road, Ascot Vale, Victoria 3032.
CANADA
The National Equestrian Federation, c/o National Sport and Recreation Association, 333 River Road, Vanier, Ontario K1L 8B9.
GERMANY
Deutsches Olympiade Kommittee für Reiterei, Freiher-von-Langen Strasse 14, 4410 Warendorf.
NEW ZEALAND
The New Zealand Horse Society, RD2 Hastings.

Glossary of terms

Aids: the means by which the rider conveys his wishes to the horse. Natural aids are the hands, body, legs and voice. Artificial aids are whips or sticks, spurs and martingales.

Bit: the mouthpiece of the bridle, usually made of metal, rubber or vulcanite, and the means by which horses are normally controlled. The reins attached to it are the means by which the rider is able to indicate his wishes to the horse.

Bitless bridle: a bridle with no bit. Control is achieved by pressure on the nose.

Blaze: a broad white mark down the front of a horse's face, usually stretching from between the eyes to the muzzle.

Breaking in: the initial training of the horse when he is ridden for the first time. This is usually carried out at three to four years old except in the case of race horses when it is done earlier.

Breastplate: a specially designed piece of tack which prevents the saddle from slipping back.

Bridoon: a thin snaffle bit usually with small rings, used in conjunction with a curb bit in a double bridle.

Cantle: the raised back of the saddle which prevents the rider from slipping too far back.

Cheek pieces: the parts of the bridle which support the bit at one end and are attached to the head piece at the other.

Chestnut: a ginger or reddish coloured horse. Also, the name given to the fifth toe of a horse which presents itself as an oval of horn just below the hocks and just above the knees. It should be kept trimmed by the blacksmith.

Colt: a young male horse up to three years of age.

Crupper: a specially designed piece of tack which prevents the saddle from slipping forward.

Curb: a type of bit with a chain, used with a bridoon bit in a double bridle. Also, the name given to a swelling caused by strain which appears about 10cm (4in) below the point of the hock.

Dock: the end of the spine which becomes the bony part of the tail.

Double bridle: a bridle with two bits, a bridoon and curb, both of which have reins attached.

Dun: a gold-coloured horse, usually with black points.

Egg-butt snaffle: a popular snaffle bit designed with rounded ends which prevent rubbing on the sides of the horse's mouth.

Entire: a stallion or uncastrated male horse.

F.E.I.: Fédération Equestre Internationale, the governing body controlling all international horse trials, show jumping and dressage events.

Filly: a young female up to three years of age.

Flea-bitten grey: a light grey horse with flecks of brown or black hairs in the coat.

Gelding: a castrated male of any age.

Girth: the strong leather, nylon or string strap which goes under the horse's belly and is attached at both ends to the saddle, to keep it in place.

Hacking: riding for pleasure out of doors.

Half bred: a horse with one thoroughbred parent.

Hock: the pointed joint on the hind leg between the gaskin or second thigh and cannon bone.

Jockeys: black grease marks which can develop on saddlery. They should be removed with coarse cloth.

List: a black line along the spine of some horses, all donkeys and many mules.

Lunging: the art of exercising or schooling the horse on a long rein on the circle, with or without a rider.

Mare: a female horse of any age.

Nearside: the left hand side of the horse when facing in the same direction.

Neck strap: a strap placed round the horse's neck, used by a rider, especially a beginner, to take hold of to retain his balance.

Offside: the right hand side of the horse when facing in the same direction.

Acknowledgments

Palomino: a gold-coloured horse with a white mane and tail.

Piebald: a black and white horse.

Points: the parts of the horse. Also, when used in conjunction to colour, black points refer to black muzzle, tips of the ears, mane, tail and the extremities of the legs.

Poll: the flat part of the head directly behind the ears.

Pommel: the top of the raised arch on the front of the saddle.

Quarters: the rump of the horse.

Roan: a colour of a horse, of which there are two kinds. Red or strawberry is a mixture of bay or chestnut and white hairs; blue is a mixture of brown or black and white hairs.

Skirt: the leather flap covering the stirrup bar on a saddle.

Splints: bony enlargements which occur usually in young horses on the cannon or splint bone. They may cause lameness while forming.

Stable rubber: a teatowel-type cloth used for dusting over a horse. Part of the grooming kit.

Stud: an establishment where horses are bred. Also, a metal plug which can be screwed into a horse's shoe to give extra grip on slippery surfaces.

Trace clip: a clip leaving the coat on the back and top half of the neck and legs.

Trimming: the means of keeping a horse neat and tidy. A trimmed horse should have a neat mane, tail, jaw and heels.

Unbroken: a horse that has not been broken to saddle and so has not been ridden.

White snip, star, stripe: white markings on a horse's face.

Withers: the raised part of the spine at the end of the neck immediately above the shoulders.

Wolf teeth: molar-type teeth which may grow and cause discomfort if they appear where the bit rests in the horse's mouth. They should be removed if they are troublesome.

The publishers would like to thank the individuals and organizations listed below for their kind permission to reproduce the following photographs in this book:

All Sport Photographic: page 48 top and bottom left (Don Morley); page 48 bottom right (Peter Greenland); page 49 top (Tony Duffy); page 49 centre row right and bottom row right (Don Morley); page 50 top (Tony Duffy); page 50 bottom right (Don Morley); page 51 (Don Morley); page 110 top left and overall photograph pages 110-111 (Peter Greenland); page 111 top left (Peter Greenland) and top right (Tony Duffy)

Blue Sky Holidays: page 28 bottom left

British Tourist Authority: page 8; pages 28-29 overall photograph plus insets bottom left and centre and right of page 29

Buriot: page 94 bottom

Jeffrey Byron: page 9 (black and white)

Eventer: page 9 (colour)

Kit Houghton Photography: page 49 centre row left

E. D. Lacey: page 49 bottom row centre; page 50 bottom left

Anthony Loriston-Clarke: page 24; page 106 top

Marston Photo-Graphics: page 83 bottom right

Spectrum Colour Library: page 110 bottom left

Trevor Spooner: pages 90-91 top

Sally Anne Thompson: page 94 top right; page 95 top left and right

Steven Williams: page 106 bottom

Photographs in the book of Jane Holderness-Roddam are reproduced with the permission of the British Equestrian Federation to whom a donation has been paid.